T0233166

# SpringerBriefs in Law

SpringerBriefs present concise summaries of cutting-edge research and practical applications across a wide spectrum of fields. Featuring compact volumes of 50 to 125 pages, the series covers a range of content from professional to academic. Typical topics might include:

- A timely report of state-of-the art analytical techniques
- A bridge between new research results, as published in journal articles, and a contextual literature review
- A snapshot of a hot or emerging topic
- A presentation of core concepts that students must understand in order to make independent contributions

SpringerBriefs in Law showcase emerging theory, empirical research, and practical application in Law from a global author community. SpringerBriefs are characterized by fast, global electronic dissemination, standard publishing contracts, standardized manuscript preparation and formatting guidelines, and expedited production schedules.

Megan Richardson

# The Right to Privacy 1914–1948

## The Lost Years

 Springer

Megan Richardson
Melbourne Law School
University of Melbourne
Carlton, VIC, Australia

ISSN 2192-855X          ISSN 2192-8568    (electronic)
SpringerBriefs in Law
ISBN 978-981-99-4500-9     ISBN 978-981-99-4498-9    (eBook)
https://doi.org/10.1007/978-981-99-4498-9

This Springer imprint is published by the registered company Springer Nature Singapore Pte Ltd.
The registered company address is: 152 Beach Road, #21-01/04 Gateway East, Singapore 189721,
Singapore

# Acknowledgements

This book suffers from a double disadvantage of being both about privacy and therefore often drawing on sources that are often by their nature 'wanting', 'silent', and 'reticent', as Michelle Perot put it in her introduction to vol IV of *The History of Private Life* (*L'Histoire de la Vie Privée*), and of a time marked by death and disruption where much of the original source material is lost or its publication is left to the judgements of intermediaries whose personal involvements in the lives of the authors exemplify the entanglements of private and public life.

As such, I have benefited immeasurably from James Underwood's Schlegel-Tieck prize-winning translation of Franz Kafka's *The Castle* based on Malcom Pasley's German critical edition of *Das Schloß* from 1982 (which I have also consulted), and Keith Tribe's excellent new edition and translation of *Economy and Society* based on Max Weber's original manuscript for *Wirtschaft und Gesellschaft*. At the same time, I have found both useful and interesting Willa and Edwin Muir's earlier translations of Kafka's text as edited by his friend and executor Max Brod, and the Talcott Parsons, AR Henderson *et al* editions/translations of Weber's text based on his wife Marianne's posthumous edition. Likewise, for Kafka's other writings which appeared in the decades after his death, I have juggled between different versions – for instance, preferring fresh translations of his letters published in Brod's edition of his *Briefe 1902-1924*, over the translations of Richard and Clara Winston, and preferring Michael Hofmann's elegant translations of Kafka's novel *Amerika* and story '*Forschungen eines Hundes*' ('Investigations of a Dog') over the Muirs' earlier translations. Also, bearing in mind the haphazard posthumous publication of Weber's and Kafka's works, in referencing this material I have moved away from the usual practice of including the date of first publication in favour of the date of completion of the manuscript (as well as the date of the translation I am using, where relevant).

Fortunately when it comes to Henri Bergson, the fact that he read and 'authorised' the translation of Arthur Mitchell of Harvard University gives greater confidence that Mitchell's editions of *Creative Evolution*, first published in London and New York in 1911, provide an adequate reflection of Bergson's own selected words in *L'Évolution créatrice* published four years earlier in Paris (and in this book I revert to the usual practice of citing both the date of publication of the original and translation). Even so, there are occasional dated expressions in that generally fine work. Thus, I have found the more recent translation of Donald Landes a very useful comparison, along with the original Paris edition of *L'Évolution créatrice*.

I owe special thanks to a range of individuals for their help and support over the course of this project. In particular, I am grateful to Julian Thomas for encouraging me to write a twentieth-century history of data rights and for many entertaining and enlightening discussions at the early stages of the project, to senior editor Lucie Bartonek for enthusiastically taking up my idea of submitting a proposal for a SpringerBrief, to Springer's anonymous reviewers for their thoughtful and constructive comments and suggestions on the proposal, to participants in conferences on 'Habsburg Civil Servants' and 'Memory, Forgetting and Creating' who heard earlier versions of Chaps. 3 and 4 and shared some very useful responses, to Rachelle Bosua and Damian Clifford for sharing their own valuable ideas and insights about the diverse relationships of technology and rights as I was finalising these chapters, and to my husband Martin Vranken for his generosity in reading sections of the manuscript and his expert advice on translations of the original German and French texts. Hartelijk dank, Martin!

Other thanks are due to institutional repositories and the individuals and communities that nourish and support them. Without the services of the Baillieu Library and Special Collections at the University of Melbourne and State Library of Victoria, with their collection histories dating back to the nineteenth century, I would not have been able to complete this project. Likewise, the University of Melbourne's Law Library gave me necessary access to its extensive holdings of human rights material, including William Schabas's three-volume edition of *The Universal Declaration of Human Rights: The Travaux Préparatoires*, published by Cambridge University Press in 2013, and Johannes Morsink's *Article by Article: The Universal Declaration of Human Rights for a New Generation*, published by the University of Pennsylvania Press in 2021, which I found especially helpful in preparing this book.

As to the original images and other original materials I have used in this book, I am grateful to the Art Institute of Chicago, the State Library of New South Wales, State Library Victoria, the National Library of Israel, *BnF Gallica*, *The Illustrated London News* (1842–2003) and *The Times Digital Archive* (1785–2014) on Gale Primary Sources, *The New York Times* (1851–2019) on ProQuest Historical Newspapers, Gutenberg Press, Internet Archive, and Wikimedia.

# About this Book

This book considers the right to privacy and contiguous rights in the years encompassing and disrupted by the twentieth century's two world wars. With many of the most interesting modern thinkers of the period dead or marginalised (or both) by 1948, their ideas about how rights such as privacy should develop to accommodate the exigencies of modern life failed to find much of a voice in the drafting of the Universal Declaration of Human Rights. Yet they anticipated in surprising ways some of our 'new' ways of thinking in more recent times.

**Keywords** Privacy · Identity · Rights · Modern · Universal declaration

# Contents

# Chapter 1
# Introduction

**Abstract** This chapter introduces the themes of the book as centred on the right to privacy and contiguous rights in the years encompassing and disrupted by the two world wars of the first half of the twentieth century. It argues that, with many of the most interesting modern thinkers of the period dead or marginalised (or both) by 1948, their ideas about how rights such as privacy should develop to accommodate the exigencies of modern life failed to find much of a voice in the drafting of the Universal Declaration of Human Rights. Yet it points out that they anticipated in surprising ways some of our 'new' ways of thinking about these rights in more recent times.

**Keywords** Privacy · Identity · Rights · Modern · Universal declaration

In 1905 Spanish philosopher and cultural critic George Santayana wrote that 'those who cannot remember the past are doomed to repeat it'.[1] Nine years later the world was at war and by the end of the next world war many of the key figures of this book were gone, along with much of the detail of their thinking about privacy and identity in modern times. Samuel Warren who inspired and co-authored the first major modern work on 'The Right to Privacy' in the 1890 Harvard Law Review,[2] was dead by suicide by 1910. His co-author Louis Brandeis, champion of privacy as well as free speech, was dead by 1941. Max Weber, author of the great twentieth century study of bureaucracy, died in Germany from Spanish flu in 1920. Franz Kafka, writer on the terrors of bureaucracy, died from tuberculosis in an Austrian sanitorium in 1924. Henri Bergson, French vitalist philosopher who inspired new ways of thinking about human freedom, died from bronchitis after queuing for registration as a Jew in occupied Paris in 1941. Hannah Arendt lived into the 1970s but in the late 1940s she was a stateless refugee escaping Germany and recently arrived in New York

---

[1] Santayana (1905), p 284.

[2] Warren and Brandeis (1890).

with very little influence on world affairs. Her friend Walter Benjamin died by suicide as a refugee from Nazi terror at the Spanish border in 1940.

By the time we came to the right to privacy's inscription in the Universal
Declaration of Human Rights in 1948, the task fell to an eclectic group of delegates
including American democratist and civil rights advocate (and widow of the US
wartime president) Eleanor Roosevelt, French jurist and expert on veteran's rights
René Cassin, Lebanese cosmopolitan and 'anti-statist' Charles Malik, and Chinese
Confucian scholar and diplomat Peng Chun Chang. The United Nations' bureaucrat, Canadian John Humphrey acted as drafter. And the president of the General
Assembly, shepherding through the final vote, was former Australian judge and
political figure Dr. Herbert Vere Evatt. The right to privacy featured in art 12 of the
Universal Declaration, alongside rights to family, home and correspondence, honour and reputation. But without a voice for deeper ideas about how the right should
develop for protection of identity in modern life, it amounted largely to a restatement – albeit a significant restatement – of the importance of privacy in a post-war
environment. In the result, most of the modern developments around the right to
privacy and contiguous rights occurred in the years since the Universal Declaration
was agreed in a rare moment of international consensus.

In some ways, the Universal Declaration with its orderly scheme of rights agreed
by committee and expressed in dry bureaucratic language, can be seen as representing
the style of modernism. Certainly, it is a far cry from the post-revolutionary declaration of utopian rights encapsulated in poet Percy Bysshe Shelley's language of 'the
gigantic shadows which futurity casts upon the present'.[3] But there is nothing of the
modernist imagination here in its treatment of privacy and contiguous rights. Its
Preamble states that 'recognition of the inherent dignity and of the equal and inalien-
able rights of all members of the human family is the foundation of freedom, justice
and peace in the world', and that 'disregard and contempt for human rights have
resulted in barbarous acts which have outraged the conscience of mankind'.[4] But the
drafting history and actual text of art 12 suggest that the more immediate practical
concern was to take a fairly traditional idea of the right to privacy, situate it alongside
contiguous rights to family, home and correspondence, as well as honour and reputation, and insert it into the Declaration in 1948 without much more.[5] Thus I want to
contest Samuel Moyn's contention, at least with respect to rights such as privacy, that
'human rights [at the time of the Declaration] were not a promise waiting to be
realized but a utopia first too vague then too conservative to matter'.[6] To the contrary,
I suggest, it was because the Declaration's framings of rights around privacy were not
modern enough in 1948 – to adapt Arendt's words, they were insufficiently 'redefined
in light of present experiences and circumstances'[7] – that so much of the work had to

---

[3] Shelley (1821) in Wu (2012), p. 1247.

[4] Universal Declaration of Human Rights (1948), Preamble, first and second recitals.

[5] Cf Morsink (2021), pp. 81–5. And see generally the *Travaux Préparatoires* in Schabas (2013).

[6] Moyn (2010), pp. 47–48.

[7] Arendt (1949), p 34.

be done afterwards in the project of conceiving rights of human identity for our current century. Nevertheless, one premise of this book is that there is still much to be gained from connecting our emerging conceptions with those being developed in earlier (i.e. pre-1948) modern times.

In the next chapter, I focus on how, under the intensely urbanised and transient conditions of modern life – what sociologist Georg Simmel referred to as "the external culture and technique of life",[8] with its appurtenant technologies of photography, cinema, telephone, radio and television, new legal questions were posed in courts of the common law world about the possibility of privacy for those made subject to the public gaze. By now based in the United States, former refugee Arendt in her early essay on 'The Right to Have Rights', published in the *Modern Review* in 1949, foreshadowed a promising expanded understanding of a 'sphere of private life in which, through friendship, sympathy and love, we can cope more or less adequately with mere human existence',[9] even outside the protective sphere of a given 'home' or 'community'.[10] This intriguing idea of a social privacy, formed around what may be fleeting relationships and with no necessary connection with designated private places, found little acknowledgment in mid-century conservative courts or, for that matter, in the Universal Declaration's right to 'privacy'. And in Arendt's later writings she moved away from this idea, becoming more intent on the value of participation in public life. But now, with experience of the internet and social media, we can see Arendt's earlier idea of social privacy echoed in a new imaginary of privacy as a sphere of human intimacy and flourishing that is capable *inter alia* of operating within fluid semi-social arrangements and semi-public settings.[11]

In the third chapter, I move on to consider how ideas of data rights going beyond privacy (at least if conceived as a right not to be subject to the public gaze) started to emerge in the 1910s and 1920s in response to bureaucratic technologies and practices. In contrast to Weber's vision of rational bureaucracy as an efficient mechanism for control of bureaucratic subjects put forward in *Economy and Society* (*Wirtschaft und Gesellschaft*),[12] Kafka in *The Castle* (*Das Schloß*)[13] drew on his surrealist imagination to explore the human vicissitudes of bureaucratic practices for the subjects of bureaucracy who ask for 'my rights' but are without rights. But Kafka also went further in his office and other writings to provide us with deep insights into how an ideal humanist bureaucracy should function. Kafka's ideas find resonances in the right to informational self-determination developed in the West German Constitutional court in the 1980s,[14] drawing on the rights to dignity and free

---

[8] Simmel (1903), p 324.

[9] Arendt (1949), pp. 32–33.

[10] Ibid, pp. 26, 28.

[11] See, for instance, Marwick and Boyd (2014); Richardson (2017); Bannerman (2019); Citron (2022).

[12] Weber (1920).

[13] Kafka (1922).

[14] Census Act Case, 65 BVerfGE 1 (1983).

development of personality spelt out in the Basic Law of 1949 (and representing a distinct step beyond the Universal Declaration)[15] – a right that is now increasingly seen as underpinning contemporary data protection laws.

In the fourth chapter, I turn to challenges posed for human identity by an increasingly pervasive and mechanised early twentieth century arts and entertainment industry dedicated to recording and replaying fictionalised accounts of human life stories for public enlightenment and entertainment. Here, I suggest, the problem was not just, as Michel Foucault described, one of organised knowledge submerging the subjugated knowledges of others,[16] but the ways that both types of knowledge may be brought together and weighed against the efforts of individual human subjects to tell their own stories. I explore how Bergson's vitalist arguments for creative self-development as opposed to 'cinematic mechanism' in his early modernist work on *Creative Evolution* (*L'Évolution créatrice*)[17] inspired a generation captivated by the Bergsonian idea of 'creativity, change and freedom'[18] – including plaintiffs and judges in diverse legal cases of the 1920s and 1930s. I argue that their reasoning takes on a new significance in developing and construing data rights around erasure/forgetting and rectification of the record in our highly mechanised and networked world which challenges forgetting and problematises distinctions between true and false, free and determined.

In the final chapter, I reflect back on ways of thinking about privacy and contiguous rights in 'modern times',[19] being times not only dominated by 'the external culture and technique of [modern] life' but also replete with novel and interesting ideas about how to maintain a sense of human identity. If, as Arendt argued, human rights are necessary mechanisms to keep humans within society,[20] then I suggest that we need to pay attention to diverse human understandings of the right to privacy and contiguous rights. The illuminations offered by those who feature in this book's investigations are still quite vague. Yet they anticipated in surprising ways 'new' ways of thinking around privacy and contiguous rights in more recent times.

## References

Arendt H (1949) 'The rights of man': what are they? Mod Rev 3(1):24–36
Bannerman S (2019) Relational privacy and the networked governance of the self. Inf Commun Soc 22(14):2187–2202
Bergson H (1907) L'Évolution créatrice (creative evolution). In: Bergson H (1912) Creative evolution (trans: Mitchell A). Macmillan, London

---

[15] German Basic Law (1949), arts 1 and 2.

[16] Foucault (1976).

[17] Bergson (1907).

[18] Herring (2019).

[19] Chaplin (1936).

[20] Arendt (1949), p. 34.

Chaplin C (1936) Modern times. United Artists, Hollywood

Citron DK (2022) The fight for privacy: protecting dignity, identity and love in the digital age. Norton, New York

Federal Republic of Germany (1949, May 23) Basic Law for the Federal Republic of Germany

Foucault M (1976) Two lectures. In Foucault M (1980), Power/knowledge: selected interviews and other writings, 1972–1977 (ed Gordon C, trans: Gordon C et al). Harvester, London, pp. 78–108

Herring E (2019, May 6) Henri Bergson, celebrity (ed Warburton N). Aeon. https://aeon.co/essays/henri-bergson-the-philosopher-damned-for-his-female-fans

Kafka F (1922) Das schloß (the castle). In: Kafka (1997) The castle (trans: Underwood J A. from Kafka F (1982) Das schloß, vol 1 (Pasley M herausgegeben). Fischer, Frankfurt am M). Penguin, London

Marwick A, Boyd D (2014) Networked privacy: how teenagers negotiate context in social media. New Media Soc 16(7):1051–1067

Morsink J (2021) Article by article: the universal declaration of human rights for a new generation. University of Pennsylvania Press, Philadelphia

Moyn S (2010) The last utopia: human rights in history. The Belknap Press of Harvard University Press, Cambridge

Richardson M (2017) The right to privacy: origins and influence of a nineteenth-century idea. Cambridge University Press, Cambridge

Santayana G (1905) The life of reason, vol 1. Scribner's, New York

Shelley PB (1821), A defence of poetry. In: Wu D (ed) (2012) Romanticism: an anthology, 4th edn. Blackwell, Oxford, pp 1233–1247

Simmel G (1903) The metropolis and mental life (Die großstädte und das geistesleben). In: Simmel G (1991) On individuality and social forms (ed Levine DN). University of Chicago Press, Chicago, pp 324–339

United Nations General Assembly (1948, December 10) Universal Declaration of Human Rights. Res 217 A(III)

Warren SD, Brandeis LD (1890) The right to privacy. Harv L Rev 4(5):193–220

Weber M (1920) Wirtschaft und gesellschaft (economy and society). In Weber M (2019) Economy and society: a new translation (ed and trans: Tribe K). Harvard University Press, Cambridge

# Chapter 2
# Reimagining Privacy in the Face of Modernism

**Abstract** This chapter focuses on how, under the intensely urbanised and transient conditions of modern life, with its appurtenant technologies of photography, cinema, telephone, radio and television, legal questions were being posed in the United States and other parts of the common law world about the possibility of privacy for those made subject to public gaze. By now based in the United States, former refugee Hannah Arendt in 1949 foreshadowed an understanding of a 'sphere of private life in which, through friendship, sympathy and love, we can cope more or less adequately with mere human existence'. This idea of a social privacy found little acknowledgment in mid-century courts or, for that matter, in the Universal Declaration's right to 'privacy'. And in Arendt's later writings she moved away from this idea, becoming more intent on participation in public life. But in today's highly mediated world, we can see Arendt's idea echoed in a 'new' language of privacy as a sphere of human intimacy and flourishing capable of operating within fluid semi-social arrangements and semi-public settings.

**Keywords** Privacy · Photography · Cinema · Radio · Modernism · Universal declaration

## 2.1 Introduction

Already in 1873 American politician James Garfield observed how '[p]ublic affairs are now more public, and private less private, than in former ages', with people living 'almost in each other's sight' – attributing this to the telegraph, the railroad and the press working together to ensure that the 'political, social and industrial events of this day, will be reported and discussed at more than two millions of American breakfast tables tomorrow morning', with 'public opinion kept in constant exercise in training – ready to approve, condemn and command'.[1] Nor was this only in

---

[1] Garfield (1880) p 3.

America although perhaps it was most extremely felt there. Thus historian Richard Menke shows how Garfield's statement virtually anticipated the media reporting of every excruciating detail of his death as president in 1881, 2 months after his shooting by Charles Julius Guiteau at a railroad station in Washington DC, utilising the affordance of the telegraph.[2] The breakdown in boundaries was further fostered with the proliferation of media and communications technologies in ensuing decades, including portable photography, cinema, wireless telegraphy, radio and television.[3] In this chapter, I suggest that the changes produced effects not only for the legal protection of privacy but for its very character and attributes.

We see this in the reasoning of Boston lawyers Samuel Warren and Louis Brandeis, writing in the 1890 *Harvard Law Review*,[4] arguing that a different legal approach was required to the protection of privacy given the socio-technological changes. As if in response to Garfield's sanguine observation on, and lived experience of, loss of privacy, is their comment that:

> Recent inventions and business methods call attention to the next step which must be taken for the protection of the person, and for securing to the individual ... the right 'to be let alone.' Instantaneous photographs and newspaper enterprise have invaded the sacred precincts of private and domestic life; and numerous mechanical devices threaten to make good the prediction that 'what is whispered in the closet shall be proclaimed from the house-tops ...; and the question whether our law will recognize and protect the right to privacy in this and in other respects must soon come before our courts for consideration.[5]

They also had some important things to say about the character of the right to privacy in contemporary life. Much has been made of their language of a 'right to be let alone', as in the above statement. Perhaps more interestingly for present purposes, they identified it further as a right to 'the privacy of private life',[6] protecting 'the private life, habits, acts, and relations' of 'all persons',[7] 'whatsoever; their position or station',[8] from 'invasion either by the too enterprising press, the photographer, or the possessor of any other modern device for recording or reproducing scenes or sound'.[9] Even so, these prescient modern authors did not fully imagine how the nineteenth century idea of the privacy of private life, as distinct from public life,[10] would be reimagined under the impetus of new media and communications technologies.

---

[2] Menke (2020), pp. 31–40.

[3] See Beniger (1986), p 7.

[4] Warren and Brandeis (1890).

[5] Ibid, pp. 195–196.

[6] Ibid, p. 215.

[7] Ibid, p. 216.

[8] Ibid, p. 214.

[9] Ibid, p. 206.

[10] See generally Perrot (1990); Richardson (2017).

## 2.2 Photography and Cinema

That Warren and Brandeis would focus on 'instantaneous photography' as a catalyst for their arguments in 1890 is hardly surprising. Two years earlier, George Eastman established his Kodak company in Kodak Park in Rochester, New York and used this as a vehicle to mass-market his newly patented Kodak camera. The Kodak along with other portable cameras became a major influence on a growing street photography movement, embraced by amateurs as well as professionals, and dedicated to capturing the detail of modern urban life in visual form. Thus, while Garland in the 1870s had noticed how the railroad and telegraph ensured that people in America lived 'almost in each other's sight', with the invention, marketing, and popularisation of portable photography from the late 1880s onwards the public visibility of American life moved from people just living in each other's sights to the double exposure of at the same time being recorded by the one in possession of the recording equipment.

Inevitably this led to complaints about privacy. Samantha Barbas notes how a string of plaintiffs, across the United States objected to the media's 'exposure of names, photographs, and personal facts', 'a reflection of mass media's dependence on private life as a source of material'.[11] And where plaintiffs failed to receive recognition of a common law tort in court (which Barbas suggests was not unusual, despite judicial sympathy for Warren and Brandeis's arguments), the legislature might step in with a statutory tort responding to popular pressure – as with §§ 50 and 51 of the New York Civil Rights Law of 1903, prohibiting the appropriation of a person's name or likeness in trade or advertising, enacted a year after *Roberson v Rochester Folding Box Company* (1902),[12] brought by a young Abigail Roberson objecting to use of her image on advertising posters, where the New York Court of Appeal refused to declare a privacy tort covering her situation but suggested the legislature might be an appropriate vehicle. Jessica Lake notes the significance of these law reform efforts in favour of privacy being so often initiated by women.[13] Also interesting, I would say, is the fact that they were quite often initiated by women (and men) of no special position or station, and in response to scenarios taking place in public yet somehow still 'in private' caught by the watchful eye of the camera.

Of course, some things did not become the stuff of legal cases even if some of them might be objected to by those caught by the camera. For instance, Walker Evans' 'Subway Photographs', recorded surreptitiously by his 35 mm Contax camera hidden under his topcoat on the New York Subway in the late 1930s and early 1940s but only released for public exhibition at the Museum of Modern Art in 1966. As the catalogue explained, 'the photographs] are released now for the Museum exhibition because, Evans says, the 'rude and impudent invasion involved has been

---

[11] Barbas (2010), p. 195.
[12] *Roberson v Rochester Folding Box Co*, 171 NY 538, 64 NE 442 (NY Ct App, 1902).
[13] Lake (2016).

carefully softened and partially mitigated by a planned passage of time'.[14] James Agee posits that Evans's camera came closest to capturing its subjects in moments where they are 'with their guard down'.[15] Yet, being in public, we have a sense that his unwitting photographic subjects remain ever on guard against the possibility of being seen. In the words of Virginia Woolf 'the vagueness, the gleam of glassiness in [their] eyes', refracts their thoughts,[16] with each attempting (so far as they are able), per Georg Simmel, 'to maintain the independence and individuality of his existence against the sovereign powers of society'.[17]

Likewise, in Alfred Stieglitz's 'The Steerage', taken by Stieglitz on the SS Kaiser Wilhelm II from New York to Bremen, Germany in June 1907, the figures in steerage seem hardly aware that they are being snapped from the deck above in close-up detail with the aid of photographer's Auto-Graflex camera. Yet, being in a semi-public place, visible to those on the decks around and above, his subjects' expressions are tempered even while their private domestic affairs (clothes hanging on the line, babies nursed, etc.) are fully on display. Jason Francisco suggests that, enigmatic in their lack of apparent social bonds and social status, and in 'the condition between coming and going, quest and aftermath', they call out for further scrutiny and analysis.[18] But equally it might be said that this iconic modernist photograph, with its images of ordinary people of passing acquaintanceship living in close quarters during their time onboard the transatlantic ocean liner, was dedicated to capturing and exposing for public view the private lives of the steerage passengers going about their temporary daily routines (Fig. 2.1).

Naturally, given their limited status and resources, any concerns these photographic subjects might have had about Stieglitz's photography remained unvoiced, even as it was circulated to ever-wider audiences including in, first, his *Camera Work* in 1911, and later mass-circulation periodicals such as *Vanity Fair* in 1924, and the *Saturday Evening Post* in 1944.[19] But in the 1932 case of *Blumenthal v Picture Classics*,[20] the plaintiff Miriam Blumenthal, a widow peddling bread and rolls to passers-by in the lower East Side district of New York, brought proceedings seeking an injunction after she found herself featured in the defendants' motion picture 'Sightseeing in New York'.[21] Centred on comic duo Nick Basil and Tony Martin (aka Henry Ametta) in the characters of taxi drivers introducing two out-of-town female tourists to the busy lives of diverse peoples on the crowded streets of New York, with a particular focus on the Italian and Jewish quarters including

---

[14] Museum of Modern Art (1966).

[15] Agee (1966), p. 16.

[16] Woolf (1917), p. 106.

[17] Simmel (1903) in Simmel (1991), p. 324.

[18] Francisco (2012), p. 75.

[19] See Lee (2012), p. 2.

[20] *Blumenthal v Picture Classics, Inc*, 235 App Div 570; 257 NY Supp 800 (NY App. Div, 1932).

[21] Sandrich (1931).

**Fig. 2.1** Alfred Stieglitz's The Steerage, photograph made 1907, printed in or before 1913. (Public domain image, courtesy Art Institute of Chicago)

Blumenthal's lower-East Side,[22] the film is presented as a record of scenes and events in New York offered 'without exaggeration or ridicule'.[23] But featuring, as it does, the running commentary of Basil and Martin as the taxi driver-guides, performed to a backdrop of popular songs, it clearly embraces a mode of humor, exaggeration and sometimes ridicule. The plaintiff's lawyer argued that given that Blumenthal was singled out in the defendant's film as a subject of particular attention: 'there [could] be no doubt that it was the intention of the photographer to take her picture and show [her] as one of the unusual characters . . . [who] might be of interest and tend to amuse the general public'.[24]

The New York appellate court in a brief majority judgment agreed that this singling out of Blumenthal in 'front view closeup' was a breach of her right to privacy under §§ 50 and 51 of the Civil Rights Law, despite the fact that she was already 'in

---

[22] Bradley (2005), p. 460.

[23] *Blumenthal v Picture Classics*, p 572 (O'Malley J dissenting).

[24] See Lake (2016), p. 142, citing *Blumenthal v Picture Classics*, Record and Briefs ('Affidavit of Harry Roter Sworn 30 January 1932').

public view' – and that the line between news reporting and catering to the audience 'for trade purposes' had been crossed in this intrusive act of public entertainment.[25] In the American Law Institute's First Restatement of Torts, volume IV, published 7 years later the reasoning of the court in *Blumenthal*, with its broad reading the New York Civil Rights Law, was enlarged in § 867 to frame a more general tort of 'interference with privacy', framed in terms of 'a person who unreasonably and seriously interferes with another's interest in not having his affairs known to others or his likeness exhibited to the public'.[26] Although the distinguished Professor Arthur Goodhart of Oxford University observed that it was 'surprising' to see the tort framed in such categorical terms in a purported restatement of US law, given that so many states were yet to recognise this rule, he agreed that it represented the New York position.[27]

We might wonder how an American and especially a New York court would have considered the Soviet constructivist filmmaker Dziga Vertov's great modernist film of 1929, 'Man with a Movie Camera' (*Chelovek s Kinoapparatom*).[28] In this film we are exposed to full view of people in Moscow, Kyiv, and Odessa going about their daily lives under the watchful camera-eye of Vertov (aka Denis Kaufman), apparently oblivious to the eponymous movie camera being wielded by Vertov's brother Miles Kaufman. Yet we see it follow them around, zooming in and out for the benefit of the audience which seats itself at the beginning of the film, in a gloriously self-reflexive act of *cinéma verité*. The film was shown on the American screen in September 1929 and reviewed critically in the *New York Times*.[29] As film historian Lewis Jacobs records, Vertov's advocation of pictures 'without professional actors, without stories, and without artificial scenery' had great appeal to American experimental independent filmmakers of the 1930s who 'eagerly embraced' his manifesto of the film's recording of everyday life as the foundation of art, following this with 'a flock' of 'city symphonies'.[30] Quite possibly, it served as an inspiration for 'Sightseeing in New York' released just 2 years later.

Privacy is particularly challenged by the ever-observant camera in 'Man with a Movie Camera', moving restlessly from crowds of people engaged in social activities (travelling around in trams, trains and buses, attending sports events, working in factories, and so on), to close-ups of individuals engaged in intimate moments (birth, death, marriage, divorce, etc), to scenes that might be equally private and public (eg people sleeping on the street, people lying on the beach, people captured intent on watching the film). But while entertaining, the film's purpose is not just to entertain in the way of its American shadow, 'Sightseeing in New York'. A under the aegis of the Odesa Film Factory of the All-Ukrainian Photo Cinema

---

[25] *Blumenthal v Picture Classics*, p 571 (McAvoy J).

[26] American Law Institute (1939), § 867.

[27] Goodhart (1943), p. 508.

[28] Vertov (1929).

[29] Hall (1929).

[30] Jacobs (1947–1948), p. 120.

**Fig. 2.2** Still from Dziga Vertov's Chelovek s Kinoapparatom (Man with a Movie Camera), 1929. (Public domain image, courtesy Internet Archive)

Administration, its explicit purpose is propaganda. As Vertov stated in 1923, 'I am kino-eye. I am a mechanical eye. I, a machine, show you the world as only I can see it'.[31] He insisted on the tyranny of the movie camera in the hands of its operator and those involved in filming, editing and production of the film, working to inform and instruct the audience in what might best be described as an attempt not just to capture reality but to 'reconfigure the function that media in general and film in particular play in the constitution of meaning'.[32] How should the individual respond to that reconfiguration in the name of freedom and individuality? (Fig. 2.2).

## 2.3 Telephone, Radio, Television

A year before 'Man With a Movie Camera' was released in public cinemas across America, Brandeis J, by then an Associate Justice of the US Supreme Court, issued a stinging dissent tn *Olmstead v United States*.[33] He objected to unbounded state sponsored activities of surveillance of individuals which he called a breach of 'the right to privacy' under the Fourth Amendment. But here the technology was telephone rather than film, and the purpose had less to do with the constitution of meaning as with other methods of control, namely through the institution (or threat) of criminal proceedings. The plaintiff, former police officer now popular businessman

---

[31] Vertov (1923), in Michelson (1984), p. 17.

[32] Delgado (2009), p. 12.

[33] *Olmstead v United States*, 277 US 438 (1928).

and suspected bootlegger Roy Olmstead, objected to his office and home telephones being tapped and his conversations recorded by federal agents, in an effort to find evidence supporting a criminal conviction for conspiracy to violate the National Prohibition Act of 1919. The telephone was a staple in US business operations, including those of Olmstead and his co-conspirators, 'their words coursing across a web of wires connecting the city's fifty-two thousand devices (approximately one for every six citizens)'.[34] And it was also a means of more private social messaging, being used in this case not just by Olmstead but by his wife Elise. She was also a rather unlikely subject of investigation in her own right, being allegedly suspected of using the radio station that she and Olmstead had established in their Seattle home to send coded messages to his boats in her broadcasts of children's stories.[35]

Brandeis J argued that the government's tap amounted to a breach of Olmstead's right not to be subject to unreasonable search and seizure under the Fourth Amendment to the US Constitution, which he characterised as a 'right to privacy'. Although Brandeis J's reasoning did not persuade the Supreme Court, which concluded that the Fourth Amendment was concerned with activities on private property (while the tap here was placed in the public street outside Olmstead's premises), it was the position later taken up by the Court.[36] Particularly interesting is the way that Brandeis J talked about 'the right to privacy' some 30 years after his article with Samuel Warren. For now, rather than photography and the media being the focus of his discussion of the right to be 'let alone', it was the state's ability to listen in on a private conversation through the listening ear of the telephone tap – offering an early indicator of the subtle ways by which, with the progress of science, 'the most intimate occurrences of the home' may be discovered and exposed for public view, and unexpressed beliefs, thoughts and emotions' may be explored.[37] Further, we see Brandeis offering a more fluid idea of privacy, going even beyond 'the most intimate occurrences of the home', associated with the character of the telephone as a way of mediating a private conversation between individuals whatever their location, in his observation that '[w]henever a telephone line is tapped, the privacy of the persons at both ends of the line is invaded, and all conversations between them upon any subject, and although proper, confidential, and privileged, may be overheard.[38] In other words, in modern life, a novel privacy may be found in the intimacy of the conversation over the wires – but with a new vulnerability to breaches of privacy by those overhearing.

We can extrapolate from this reasoning to consider the prospect of a novel privacy, along with a new threat of invasion, being found in the experience of listening to the radio, although here the broadcast is not just to one (or a few) listeners, as with the telephone, but to wider and more diverse publics. We already have the

---

[34] See Abbott (2017).

[35] See Schneider (2013), pp. 20–2.

[36] The Court's shift occurring in *Katz v United States*, 389 US 347 (1967).

[37] *Olmstead v United States*, p 474 (Brandeis J).

[38] Ibid, pp. 475–6.

example of Elise Olmstead who experimented with the radio as a popular medium for her persona 'Aunt Vivian' reading bedtime stories to children in the Seattle area in the 1920s, sandwiching this between the night-time news, weather and stock broadcasts and 'live' performances of the Earl Gray Orchestra at the Butler Hotel café in downtown Seattle, but also carefully monitored by federal agents. According to Walter Benjamin, who wrote and delivered on German radio more than 80 popular educational programs for young people between 1927 and 1933, radio's unique capability as a technology lies in its ability to engage directly with 'the so-called audience sociology',[39] minimising the separation between performer and audience.[40] On this account, radio was well poised in the 1930s not only to transmit ideas, information and conversations to people in homes, offices and more public places through thin air, but to capitalise on new possibilities for engagement and intimacy that it creates with listeners. Of course, that already would have been obvious to Benjamin, whose radio stories and plays featured 'bootleggers, or 'American alcohol smugglers' with their clever smuggling tricks to evade the prohibition law,[41] along with microphones installed under the bed and information recorded by clever radio technicians.[42] Already he could see that this remarkable social technology created new opportunities for surveillance not only of its publics but of a whole range of others subjected to its intrusions.

But nor was it just the state that might be involved on the side of surveillance. Businesses along with their publics might be equally implicated. Interestingly, the leading case of the mid-twentieth century on this point was an Australian case, *viz* the 1937 case of *Victoria Park Racing & Recreation Grounds Co Ltd v Taylor.*[43] What it shows is that, if anything, Australian like English law was even further behind US law in adapting to the impacts of new technologies of watching and listening when it came to the settled boundaries of privacy law.[44] Yet there were some who would like that to change, as shown by the split in the various judgments of the High Court of Australia, and the efforts of the dissenting judges in particular to frame this a case about modern privacy. On its face though it was an unlikely case about privacy, involving as it did a simple scenario of radio broadcasts of sports racing, a national pastime, by a radio station which having been denied a right to broadcast races from within the race ground arranged for its commentators to do so from high viewing platforms on a neighbour's property. But in the background was a social change taking place in Australia with radio taking on the mantle of 'conjuring up a world it shared with listeners – the everyday, ordinary, intimate world', drawing 'the citizens of the city and the outback into the national family'.[45] And the

---

[39] Benjamin (1932b), p. 371.

[40] Benjamin (1930a/1931), p. 363.

[41] Benjamin (1930b), pp. 139–144.

[42] Benjamin (1932a), p. 219.

[43] *Victoria Park Racing and Recreation Grounds Co Ltd v Taylor* (1937) 58 CLR 479.

[44] Cf Goodhart (1943), p. 508.

[45] Griffen-Foley (2007), pp. 123–132, 124.

popular 2UW commentator Cyril Angles who stood on the stand on Taylor's land and *via* telephone described the races on the race ground next door 'in a particularly vivid manner' represented this shift (Fig. 2.3).[46]

The majority judges quickly enough dispensed with the race ground's argument of invasion of privacy raised on behalf of those attending the races. As Latham CJ put it, there was no 'general right to privacy' in English and therefore Australian law, the tort of nuisance (which the plaintiff relied on) therefore did not extend to give a remedy here, and the plaintiff if concerned about the privacy of those at the races could simply build a higher fence.[47] Dixon J for his part emphasised the immutability of 'long-established rules of law'.[48] But, in dissent, Evatt J argued for a flexible approach to the law of nuisance based on loss of enjoyment of the race-ground due to the experience of being systematically overlooked,[49] while Rich J suggested that television especially presented an urgent need to consider the ways in which the private 'doings of the individual' may be threatened by the technology – virtually echoing Brandeis J in *Olmstead* in his comment that with the advance

**Fig. 2.3** Cyril Angus (racing commentator at station 2UW, Sydney). (Photographer Sam Hood, 1937, public domain image courtesy State Library of New South Wales)

---

[46] Ibid, p. 492 (per Latham CJ).

[47] See *Victoria Park Racing v Taylor*, pp. 495–6 (Latham CJ); pp. 507–8 (Dixon J); pp. 525–6 (McTiernan J).

[48] Ibid, p. 505 (Dixon J).

[49] Ibid, p. 520 (Evatt J).

of '[the] art', protection against 'the complete exposure of the doings of the individual may be a right indispensable to the enjoyment of life'.[50]

Yet even these more far-thinking dissenters' ideas about privacy still seem tied to older ideas about overlooking of private places and fixed relationships. For Evatt J, the law is (or should be) engaged when a person 'creates or uses devices for the purpose of enabling the public generally to overlook or spy upon the premises of another person', while for Rich J the underlying principle is one of 'the ordinary comfort of human existence and the ordinary enjoyment of the house beset'.[51] In short, illuminating as these judicial statements are about the need for a flexible approach to the legal protection of privacy in the face of new media and communications technologies, they still did not quite capture the ways in which the very concept of 'enjoyment of life' itself might change in the process – moving outside the traditional contours of private life kept separate from public life, to capture a more nebulous and ephemeral sphere of social privacy weaving through the sports fan community and encompassing not just those at the races but also to some extent those listening in (and later, with television, watching on), or at least to the extent found socially acceptable.

## 2.4 Echoing Arendt's Vision of Social Privacy

In 1948 Dr. Herbert Vere Evatt was elected President of the United Nations General Assembly. By then he was no longer a judge of the Australian High Court, having resigned in 1940 to stand for Parliament. As Minister for External Affairs in the post-war Labor Government, he represented the Australian delegation in the negotiations for a new post-war United Nations at its originating conference in San Francisco in 1945 where he helped craft the United Nations Charter. As such, he was intimately involved in the instigation of the fledgling United Nations' Universal Declaration of Human Rights, some version of which had been on the United Nations program from the beginning. But, as to the terms of the Declaration, this was predominantly the work of the Commission on Human Rights chaired by American Eleanor Roosevelt, widow of US wartime president Franklin D Roosevelt with Canadian John Humphrey from the secretariate responsible for the various drafts of the drafting committee in the lead up to approval of the General Assembly session in December 1948. Others closely involved in the drafting process included French-Jewish jurist and expert on veterans' rights René Cassin,[52] Chinese Confucian scholar and diplomat Peng Chun Chang,[53] Lebanese cosmopolitan and

---

[50] Ibid, p. 505 (Rich J).

[51] Ibid, p. 504 (Rich J); p. 521 (Evatt J).

[52] See Winter and Prost (2013).

[53] See Roth (2018).

'anti-statist' Charles Malik,[54] and Indian feminist Hansa Mehta.[55] (Mehta is widely credited with changing the phrase "All men are born free and equal" in the to "All human beings are born free and equal" in the Declaration's Preamble – although, to be precise, the UK-Indian proposed amendment was for 'all people' to replace 'all men' and the language of 'all human beings' came from Belgium.)[56] It is probably fair to say that that thinking about the nature and value of privacy in modern life was not the highest priority for any of these negotiators.

Instead, art 12 of the Declaration offers a rather conventional provision about privacy as sitting comfortably alongside family, home and correspondence, along with honour and reputation. Humphrey in his initial draft took the American Law Institute's draft International Bill of Rights of 1948 as a model.[57] The ALI draft's goal was itself a fairly modest one of eliciting common ideas about human rights from 'the liberal elements of the major cultures'.[58] And, as a conventional statement, its provision about privacy in art 6, headed 'freedom from wrongful interference', seemed successful, with most of the debate on art 12 in the *Travaux Préparatoires* concerning wrangling about wording not the basic ideas (Table 2.1).[59]

The Universal Declaration, including its art 12 right to privacy ('*la vie privée*' in the French version), represented a remarkable moment of consensus within the Human Rights Commission and wider body of the United Nations. And, if we may wonder about art 12's imaginary compass, there was little to challenge this in the Declaration's immediate aftermath. One of the first steps taken by the fledgling United Nations was a Travelling Exhibition under the auspices of the United Nations Educational, Scientific and Cultural Organization in 1950, based on a Paris Exhibition the previous year, whose purpose was to 'help carry the Human Rights message in visual form to the peoples of many countries'.[60] Here we see rights

**Table 2.1**  Drafting origins of Universal Declaration of Human Rights

| American Law Institute, Statement of Essential Human Rights (1948) | Universal Declaration of Human Rights (1948) |
| --- | --- |
| **Article 6 Freedom from Wrongful Interference** | **Article 12** |
| Freedom from unreasonable interference with his person, home, reputation, privacy, activities, and property is the right of every one | No one shall be subjected to arbitrary interference with his privacy, family, home or correspondence, nor to attacks upon his honour and reputation |
| The state has a duty to protect this freedom | Everyone has the right to the protection of the law against such interference or attacks |

---

[54] See Mitoma (2010).

[55] See Bhagavan (2010).

[56] Morsink (2021), p. 20.

[57] Humphrey (1984), p. 32. And cf. American Law Institute (1948), art 6 and art 12 Universal Declaration (1948).

[58] Simpson (2001), pp. 196–7.

[59] Cf Morsink (2021), pp. 81–5. And see generally the *Travaux Préparatoires* in Schabas (2013).

[60] *UNESCO Courier* (1950), p. 4.

around expression and communication, but not around privacy, presented as shaped by modern technologies like television, cinema, telephone and radio.[61] And, against the Exhibition's depictions of settled domestic arrangements centred on home and family, including one image of Roosevelt at home with her family (which, as Hilary Charlesworth points out, dates back to 1919 and papers over the Roosevelts' unconventional relationship),[62] the modern experience of millions of people whose lives have been disrupted by war seems hardly to be noticed. Rather, their experience seems better caught by Hannah Arendt who, recently arrived as a refugee in New York and writing a scathing review of the Universal Declaration in her article on 'The Right to Have Rights' in the 1949 *Modern Review*, where she argues that human rights are necessary mechanisms to keep humans within society, identifies a 'sphere of private life in which, through friendship, sympathy and love, we can cope more or less adequately with mere human existence'.[63] And she hints that, while this sphere may be rendered less 'normal' in the face of loss of 'home' and settled 'community',[64] it can continue albeit in a different form.

What form of private life did Arendt have in mind writing here in the 1940s? In her earlier article 'We Refugees' in the 1943 *Menorah Journal*, she suggests there can still be friendship and community (talking of '*we* refugees'),[65] and 'private existences with individual destinies'.[66] The language gives a glimpse of what she might have been imagining at this most transient point of her life. But it is quickly gone. She revisited her discussion of private life when her essay on 'The Right to Have Rights' was incorporated into *Totalitarianism* in 1951, followed by *The Human Condition* in 1958. By now established as a public figure in the United States, in these books she reverts to a more basic understanding of private life as one in which the individual is 'single, unique, unchangeable':[67] suggesting that private life may enrich public life by making it less 'shallow',[68] but has no greater social significance.[69] Even so, her writings from the 1940s capture, I would say, something important in the diverse understandings of social privacy embraced by those of the twenty-first century who, in the words of Eric Hobsbawm, live in multiple worlds – 'in their own, in that of the country of immigration, and in the global world which is made the common property of humanity by technology and the modern capitalist consumer and media society'.[70] Indeed, given that media society is now so all-pervasive, the idea of privacy as social probably speaks to a great many more of us.[71]

---

[61] UNESCO (1950).

[62] Charlesworth (2021), p. 187.

[63] Arendt (1949), pp. 32–34.

[64] Ibid, pp. 26, 28.

[65] See Arendt (1943), pp. 264–265 and passim.

[66] Ibid, p. 269.

[67] Arendt (1951, p. 296.

[68] Arendt (1958), p. 71.

[69] See (critically) Roessler (2005) pp. 108–109.

[70] Hobsbawm (2000), in Hobsbawm (2013), p. 28.

[71] See, for instance, Marwick and boyd (2014); Richardson (2017); Bannerman (2019); Citron (2022).

# References

Abbott K (2017, July 5) The bootlegger, the wiretap, and the beginning of privacy. New York

Agee J (1966) Introduction. In: Walker Evans (2004) Many are called. Yale University Press, New Haven

American Law Institute (1939) Restatement (first) of torts, Vol IV, § 867

American Law Institute (1948) Statement of essential human rights. In: American Law Institute (2016) 243 ANNALS of the American Academy of Political and Social Science, pp 18–26

Arendt H (1943) We refugees. In: Hannah Arendt (2007) The Jewish writings (ed Kohn J, Feldman RH). Schocken, New York, pp 264–274

Arendt H (1949) 'The rights of man': what are they? Modern Rev 3(1):24–36

Arendt H (1951) The origins of totalitarianism. Harcourt Brace, New York

Arendt H (1958) The human condition. University of Chicago Press, Chicago

Bannerman S (2019) Relational privacy and the networked governance of the self. Inf Commun Soc 22(14):2187–2202

Barbas S (2010) The death of the public disclosure tort. Yale J Law Human 22(2):171–215

Beniger J (1986) The control revolution: technological and economic origins of the information society. Harvard University of Press, Cambridge

Benjamin W (1930a) The bootleggers. In: Benjamin W (2014) Radio Benjamin (ed Rosenthal L, trans: Lutes J, Harries Schumann L, Reese DK). Verso, London, pp 139–144

Benjamin W (1930b/1931) Reflections on radio. In: Benjamin W (2014) Radio Benjamin (ed Rosenthal L, trans: Lutes J, Harries Schumann L, Reese DK). Verso, London, pp 363–364

Benjamin W (1932a) Much ado about Kasper. In: Benjamin W (2014) Radio Benjamin (ed Rosenthal L, trans: Lutes J, Harries Schumann L, Reese DK). Verso, London, pp 201–220

Benjamin W (1932b) Reflections on radio. In: Benjamin W (2014) Radio Benjamin (ed Rosenthal L, trans: Lutes J, Harries Schumann L, Reese DK). Verso, London, pp 365–368

Bhagavan M (2010) A new hope: India, the United Nations and the making of the Universal Declaration of Human Rights. Mod Asian Stud 44(2):311–347

Bradley EM (2005) The first Hollywood sound shorts 1926–1931. McFarland, Jefferson

Charlesworth H (2021) The travels of human rights: the UNESCO human rights exhibition 1950–1953. In: Chalmers S, Pahuja S (eds) Routledge handbook of international law and the humanities. Routledge, Abingdon, Oxon, pp 173–190

Citron DK (2022) The fight for privacy: protecting dignity, identity and love in the digital age. Norton, New York

Delgado S (2009) Dziga Vertov's 'Man with a Movie Camera' and the phenomenology of perception. Film Crit 34(1):1–16

Francisco J (2012) The prismatic fragment. In: Francisco J, McCauley EA (eds) The Steerage and Alfred Stieglitz. University of California Press, Berkeley, pp 66–112

Garfield JA (1880) The futures of the republic: its dangers and its hopes, address delivered before the Literary Society of Hudson College, June 2nd, 1873. George F Nesbitt & Co, New York

Goodhart AL (1943) Restatement of the law of torts, volume four: a comparison between English and American law. Law Q Rev 91(6):487–516

Griffen-Foley B (2007) Modernity, intimacy and early Australian commercial radio. In: Damousi J, Deacon D (eds) Talking and listening in the age of modernity: essays on the history of sound. ANU Press, Canb, pp 123–132

Hall M (1929) The screen. New York Times

Hobsbawm E (2000) A century of cultural symbiosis. In: Hobsbawm E (2013) Fractured times: culture and society in the twentieth century. Little Brown, London, pp 20–33

Humphrey JP (1984) Human rights and the United Nations: a great adventure. Transnational, New York

Jacobs L (1947–1948) Experimental cinema in America (part one: 1921–1941). Hollywood Q 3(2):111–124

Lake J (2016) The face that launched a thousand lawsuits: the American women who forged a right to privacy. Yale University Press, New Haven

Lee AW (2012) Introduction. In: Francisco J, McCauley EA (eds) The Steerage and Alfred Stieglitz. University of California Press, Berkeley, pp 1–15

Marwick A, Boyd D (2014) Networked privacy: how teenagers negotiate context in social media. New Media Soc 16(7):1051–1067

Menke R (2020) Literature, print culture, and media technologies, 1880–1900: many inventions. Cambridge University of Press, Cambridge

Mitoma G (2010) Charles H Malik and human rights: notes on a biography. Biography 33(1):222–241

Morsink J (2021) Article by article: the universal declaration of human rights for a new generation. University of Pennsylvania Press, Philadelphia

Museum of Modern Art (1966, October 5) Walker Evans' subway. Press release. https://www.moma.org/momaorg/shared/pdfs/docs/press_archives/3761/releases/MOMA_1966_July-December_0067_118.pdf

Perrot M (ed) (1990) From the fires of revolution to the Great War (De la révolution à la Grande Guerre, 1987) (trans: Goldhammer A). In: Ariès P, Duby G (ed) A history of private life (histoire de la vie privée), vol 4. Belknap, Cambridge

Richardson M (2017) The right to privacy: origins and influence of a nineteenth-century idea. Cambridge University Press, Cambridge

Roessler B (2005) The value of privacy (trans: RDV Glasgow). Polity, London

Roth HI (2018) PC chang and the universal declaration of human rights. University of Pennsylvania Pres, Philadelphia

Sandrich M (1931) Sightseeing in New York. Picture Classics, Hollywood

Schabas WA (ed) (2013) The universal declaration of human rights: the Travaux Préparatoires. Cambridge University Press, Cambridge

Schneider JF (2013) Seattle radio. Arcadia

Simmel G (1903) The metropolis and mental life (Die großstädte und das geistesleben). Ian: Simmel G (1991) On individuality and social forms (ed Levine DN). University of Chicago Press, Chicago, pp 324–339

Simpson AWB (2001) Human rights and the end of Empire: Britain and the genesis of the European convention. Oxford University Press, Oxford

UNESCO (1950) Human rights: exhibition album. UNESCO, Paris

UNESCO Courier (1950) Human rights message will Be spread by travelling exhibition. UNESCO Courier 3 (February 1): 4

United Nations General Assembly (1948, December 10) Universal Declaration of Human Rights. Res 217 A(III)

Vertov D (1923) The council of three. In: Vertov D (1984), Kino Eye: the writings of Dziga Vertov (ed O'Brien K, intro Michelson A). University of California Press, Berkeley, pp 14–21

Vertov D (1929) Man with a movie camera, All-Ukrainian Photo Cinema Administration

Warren SD, Brandeis LD (1890) The right to privacy. Harv Law Rev 4(5):193–220

Winter J, Prost A (2013) René Cassin and human rights: from the great war to the universal declaration. Cambridge University of Press, Cambridge

Woolf V (1917) The mark on the wall. In: Woolf V (1921) Monday or Tuesday. Harcourt, Brace, New York, pp 99–116

# Chapter 3
# Asking for Data Rights in *The Castle*

**Abstract** This chapter considers how ideas of data rights going beyond privacy (at least if conceived as a right not to be subject to the public gaze) started to emerge in the 1910s and 1920s in response to bureaucratic technologies and practices. In contrast to Max Weber's vision of rational bureaucracy as an efficient mechanism for control of bureaucratic subjects put forward in *Economy and Society* (*Wirtschaft und Gesellschaft*), Franz Kafka in *The Castle* (*Das Schloß*) drew on his surrealist imagination to explore the human vicissitudes of bureaucratic practices for the subjects of bureaucracy who ask for 'my rights' but are without rights. But Kafka also went further in his office and other writings to provide us with deep insights into how an ideal humanist bureaucracy should function. Kafka's ideas find resonances in the right to informational self-determination developed in the West German Constitutional court in the 1980s, drawing on the rights to dignity and free development of personality spelt out in the Basic Law of 1949 (and representing a distinct step beyond the Universal Declaration) – a right that is now increasingly seen as underpinning contemporary data protection laws.

**Keywords** Identity · Data rights · Weber · Kafka · Universal declaration · German basic law

## 3.1 Introduction

Along with symbolism, futurism, dadaism, surrealism and expressionism and all the other 'isms' of modernism, was the rise of what we might call bureaucratism. Before, bureaucracy was a necessary fact of life, an adjunct to a mechanised and utilitarian society albeit one that was occasionally critiqued and resisted – as in Charles Dickens' objections to the binds of 'office-pens' and 'red tape' in *David*

M. Richardson, *The Right to Privacy 1914–1948*, SpringerBriefs in Law,
https://doi.org/10.1007/978-981-99-4498-9_3

*Copperfield*,[1] Melville's quietly rebellious 'Bartleby the Scrivener',[2] and Jules Verne's eerily dystopian *Paris in the Twentieth Century (Paris au XXe siècle)*,[3] with its 'litanies of Holy Accountancy' recorded in the great Ledger.[4] But with modernism it entered a new phase. Now in the early decades of the twentieth century, shaped not only by modern media and communications technologies discussed in the previous chapter but by automated punch cards,[5] the assembly line,[6] and office filing systems,[7] bureaucracy for many modernists became a symbol of the intense alienation of modern existence. At the same time, there were others who talked about bureaucracy in more 'rational' terms. Indeed, for the German sociologist Max Weber, rationally speaking, 'there is only a choice between 'bureaucratisation' and the 'dilettantism' of administration'.[8] That might have been said by English political economist and philosopher John Stuart Mill in the nineteenth century, pointing to the merits of a professional bureaucracy in the Victorian political system.[9] However, Mill's was not the modernist view of bureaucracy.

Data, enmeshed with technology, formed an essential aspect of Weber' vision of an 'ideal', by which he meant 'rational', bureaucracy. This is clear from Weber's *Economy and Society (Wirtschaft und Gesellschaft)*, published 2 years after his sudden death from Spanish flu in 1920, with the aid of his wife and fellow sociologist Marianne Weber. As Weber puts it there, the main source of the superiority of bureaucratic administration in efficiency terms lies in the role of 'specialised knowledge', which, through the development of modern technologies and economic methods of the production of goods, has been rendered 'entirely indispensable'.[10] There are a number of further aspects that Weber identifies with rational bureaucracy: including a strict distinction drawn between public 'bureaucratised' and private life – with the latter clearly viewed in distinctly old-fashioned nostalgic terms of a sphere of life kept-separate from public life ('the workplace, the office, is separated from the home')[11]; 'functionally specific separation of powers',[12] and provision made for supervision and monitoring in accordance with the rule of law especially where 'the legal type is … developed' to ensure that 'rule can take place only according to rules'.[13] But ultimately the defining feature is 'rule through

---

[1] Dickens (1850), p. 533.
[2] Melville (1853).
[3] Verne (1863).
[4] Ibid, p. 70.
[5] See Heide (2009), ch. 1.
[6] Littler (1978).
[7] See Vismann (2000).
[8] Ibid, p. 351.
[9] See Warner (2001).
[10] Weber (1920), p. 351.
[11] Ibid, p. 345.
[12] Ibid, p. 425.
[13] Ibid, p. 411.

knowledge' that only a fully professional, specialist, rule-bound bureaucracy can provide.[14]

We can see here that in the bureaucratised part of human life talked about by Weber, there was little scope for free flourishing of human personality. Rather, as Weber saw it, modern bureaucracy's tide of 'rationalization and intellectualization' would lead inevitably to the submerging of human personality.[15] Anyway, he was not an advocate of the modern cult of 'personality', or the 'fanaticism' of rights.[16] Even so, I point out in this chapter that Weber's modernist contemporaries had radically different ideas of the actual and possible relationships of bureaucracy and human identity. Most significantly, there was Franz Kafka, German-Bohemian Jew, reluctant Worker's Accident Insurance Institute functionary, and writer of surrealist fictions who died of tuberculosis in in Austria in June 1924. According to John Hamilton, Kafka prefigured the surrealists' inspiration of bureaucracy as a sources of informational power to be interrogated and subverted.[17] And this was especially, I would say in his great unfinished novel, *The Castle* (or *Das Schloß*) from 1922.[18] Kafka's ideas, moving beyond Weber's, can do much to inform our conflicted and still-evolving idea of a right to data protection as not just concerned with 'rule of law', but as a right of personality.

## 3.2   Weber Versus Kafka on Bureaucracy

As several scholars have noted,[19] an important connection point between Weber and Kafka can be found in Alfred Weber, Max's younger brother and a professor at the German University of Prague where Kafka studied, and chair of the examination panel for his PhD in law. In his 1910 essay on 'The Civil Servant' ('*Der Beamte*'), published in the German literary magazine *Der Neue Rundschau*, Alfred Weber offered a trenchant critique of 'today's bureaucratization of society', or the 'new mechanization of life', decrying it as a 'gigantic problem'.[20] Indeed, he argued, in Germany already it was impacting not only the workplace but 'all other organizations of our society': ensuring that 'objectively alienated labour, and the vanishing of personality' become 'universally 'consecrated'.[21] One can see many parallels between the humanistic concerns of Alfred Weber's essay and Kafka's own writings – although Alfred Weber was more focussed on the civil servant caught up in

---

[14] Ibid, p. 352.

[15] Weber (1917), p. 133.

[16] Ibid, pp. 81, 114.

[17] Hamilton (2023).

[18] Kafka (1922a).

[19] For instance, Litowitz (2011), p. 48; Jørgensen (2012), p. 194.

[20] A Weber (1910).

[21] Ibid, p. 55.

the bureaucratic system, while Kafka's fictional writings were geared more to the insights and experiences of the bureaucratic subject. However, Kafka had his own significant knowledge of the workings of bureaucracy gleaned from his 14 years working as a civil servant at the Workman's Accident Insurance Institute in Prague ending up as a senior secretary, as a patient seeking treatment for the tuberculosis that eventually killed him in the various sanitoria of the Habsburg Empire, and as a citizen of the crumbling bureaucratic Empire in the years encompassing the first world war, all funnelled through his surrealist imagination (Fig. 3.1).

We see Kafka's vision of bureaucracy as a social institution geared closely to human nature (and subject to its impulses) in Kafka's comment to his friend Oskar Baum in June 1922:

> I have the passport, how wonderful is the new reform for the issuing of passports. It is impossible to fully grasp how bureaucracy increases as if in a necessary and unavoidable way even while it originates in human nature, to which, in my opinion, bureaucracy is

**Fig. 3.1** (From left to right) The Workmen's Accident Insurance Institute in Prague (author alphabet55, cca-sa 3.0 licence, courtesy Wikimedia), detail; Kafka photograph circa 1923/1924. (Photograph anonymous author, Archiv Frans Wagenbach, public domain, courtesy National Library of Israel)

closer than any other social institution. To describe this in detail would be too longwinded, for you in particular ....[22]

But even early on, in a letter to his friend Max Brod in August 1909, shortly after he started at the Institute, Kafka observes how humans are drivers of bureaucratic practice, when he says:

I have so much to do! In my four districts – quite apart from my other work – people fall like drunks off the scaffolding, [or] inside the machine, all beams give way, all embankments collapse, all ladders slide, what is put up falls down, what is handed down is stumbled over. And I get headaches from those young girls in the porcelain factories who constantly throw themselves off the steps with stacks of dishes.[23]

Some might think the putting together of industrial accidents with bureaucratic insurance systems would lead to a more systematic and scientific approach to the treatment of accidents, in the way of Weber's predictions of the development of rational bureaucracy. As Benno Wagner puts it, '[i]n the age of social statistics and insurance, accident develops a second mode of existence: not only as an individual fate but also as a statistical function'.[24] But, as the above snippets show, it could equally work the other way around with bureaucrats subjected to the random humanising effects of those they deal with, in particular for Kafka the accident victims he was called on to process and of course himself as a bureaucratic subject at significant points in his own life.[25] Given Kafka's propensity to refract his personal as well as professional bureaucratic existence into his fictional activities, the place to start here is his fictional writings.

Consider, for instance, Kafka's account of the experiences of his human protagonist 'K' the would-be bureaucrat in *The Castle*,[26] written when Kafka, on leave from the Institute, is convalescing at the mountain spa resort of *Spindlermühle* in the last stages of his illness.[27] In Kafka's story 'K' arrives in a village and finds a place to rest at an inn near the bridge, is denoted a land surveyor in a mysterious telephone call and sets out to the village's castle on the hill to receive his permit, but, against the weight of a bureaucratic apparatus which confirms then rescinds his authority and loses his file, struggles to gain acknowledgement of his role or his right to be in the village. As Torben Beck Jørgensen argues, in *The Castle* we see that 'Max Weber's and Franz Kafka's respective understandings of bureaucracy are as different as night and day.'[28] Yet, for Kafka, the failings seem not just the result of bureaucracy *per se*, but the result of the man-made elements of bureaucracy engaging with its systems and structures.

---

[22] Kafka (1902–1924), p. 377.

[23] Kafka (1902–1924), p. 73.

[24] Wagner, (2006), p. 97.

[25] See Kafka (1909–1917).

[26] Kafka (1922b).

[27] See Duttlinger (2017), p. 1.

[28] Jørgensen (2012), p. 194.

To begin with, in *The Castle* there are far many documents, spilling out of filing cabinets and bedroom cupboards and falling over floors in Kafka's ironic account of the vicissitudes of a would-be bureaucratic worker who is unable to move beyond his unwanted role as a mere bureaucratic subject in the village. Officials seem trapped rather than enabled by the weight of their authority, unable to draw any knowledge from their files or to exercise any definitive judgement. Moreover, the complex hierarchies of the castle seem to do nothing to ensure that rules about rule are established and monitored, with the 'control bureaux' equally given to second-guessing each other as the original bureaucrat they are called into investigate. K himself is powerless in the face of these machinations. Despite his asking for 'my rights' ('*mein Recht*'),[29] he clearly has no rights. The villagers, for their part, strive to ignore the castle's looming presence in their daily lives in the village but cannot overlook its intrusions any more than they can avoid the 'monotonous tinkling' of its bells.[30] But their behaviour towards K is equally unhelpful with their constant interactions, easy-goingness and apparent goodwill, treating him not (as he would have liked) as a formally accepted official land-surveyor with all the attendant statuses, but as someone reduced to 'the non-official, wholly unclear, clouded alien life-sphere'.[31] Moreover, public and private life and relations are completely jumbled up in K's experiences in the village under thrall of its castle – from the first telephone call from a telephone above K's bed at the first inn he stays at, to the sharing of quarters with his superior Klamm at the second one, and sleeping with Klamm's mistress Frieda. Indeed, as Kafka has 'K' reflect, '[n]owhere before had K seen officialdom and life as interwoven ['*verflochten*'] as they were here, so interwoven that it sometimes even looked as if officialdom and life had changed places'.[32] Likewise, the Weberian idea of separation of powers is neatly parodied by Kafka with the figure of the secretary Bürgel in *The Castle* indicating that in his jaundiced view, avoiding rather than engaging with responsibility should be a secretary's essential aim, even where this leads to manifestly absurd results – 'he simply, regarding things outside his competence, has no time, not so much as a moment can he spend on them'.[33]

In these various instances we see that what Kafka offers is a deep appreciation of the human dimensions of bureaucracy in all its forms. In Kafka's literary creation *The Castle*, the Weberian orderly mechanistic bureaucracy is transformed into a machine made not to work under the weight of all the frailties and excesses of the bureaucrats and their masters. Yet he is seemingly less concerned than Weber with how bureaucracy can be ordered to work, and more with the effects of bureaucracy as experienced by its human subjects. Thus, in response to the town's mayor's wondering how to avoid multiplying the same bureaucratic errors with the 'control

---

[29] Kafka (1922a), p. 67.

[30] Ibid, p. 15.

[31] Ibid, pp. 52–53.

[32] Ibid, p. 53.

[33] Ibid, pp. 236–237.

bureau' responsible for checking forming the same judgements, K retorts 'that's as may be' but he'd 'really rather not get involved in such considerations just yet'.[34] In what can be read as a considered response to Weberian rational bureaucracy, he goes on to say:

> It's just that I think two things need to be distinguished here, first what goes on inside the offices and is then capable of this or that official interpretation, and second my actual person, I who stand outside the offices and am threatened by the offices with an interference so nonsensical that I am still unable to believe in the seriousness of the danger. With regard to the first, what you tell me, sir, with such amazing and extraordinary expertise, is doubtless true, only I should like subsequently to hear something about myself as well.[35]

## 3.3 Kafka's Reformist Imagination

However, we cannot just leave it there. Given Kafka's concern with the human self 'threatened by the offices', it is not unreasonable to expect Kafka to turn his own extraordinary imagination to the question of reform. He was, after all, an acknowledged expert in the 'vast machinery of officialdom', as Walter Benjamin put it[36] – adding: '[t]he world of offices and registries ... is Kafka's world'.[37] Or per Hannah Arendt, Kafka's uniquely appreciated 'the true nature of the thing called bureaucracy'.[38] And looking across Kafka's diverse writings, there is a sense of a reformist imagination at work here. Consider, for instance, the following examples.

### 3.3.1 Adapting Bureaucracy to Accommodate Needs of Bureaucratic Subjects

One early example comes from Kafka's selected *Office Writings*, drawn from his time at the Institute and taking the form of a memorandum apparently drafted by Kafka for inclusion in the Workman's Accident Insurance Institute's Annual Report in 1909.[39] Here Kafka sets out in some detail the Institute's creative response in translating for public consumption the Habsburg Government's 1908 law designating automobile owners employing chauffeurs as 'firms' for insurance purposes and hence giving legal insurance rights to drivers. Carefully putting aside any irony of a private owner of an automobile being designated 'a firm' for legal purposes, Kafka instead emphasises the benevolent purpose of the law as being designed to address

---

[34] Ibid, p. 59.

[35] Ibid.

[36] Benjamin (1938), p. 141.

[37] Benjamin (1934), p. 112.

[38] Arendt (1944), p. 74.

[39] Kafka (1909–1917), pp. 80–86.

the practical problem of 'a group of drivers [being] exposed to danger arising from an activity in the personal interest of their employers' and highlights the Institute's response to this shift as 'an example of the flexibility and capability of the organization of the Institute, though it was originally established for different purposes'.[40] He also details the deployment of a questionnaire designed to gauge the experience of firms and provide an educative response to the problem of motor accidents, including instalment in automobiles of first-aid equipment.[41] In sum, Kafka in this early office memorandum offers an example of a model institutional response in adapting to the challenge of providing insurance against motor accidents,[42] focused on to ensuring the law's purposes are given effect and understanding the needs of its subjects, if necessary going above and beyond the strict requirements of the organisation – a response far removed from that of the secretary Bürgel in *The Castle* that if the matter is not within his competence he 'has no time, not so much as a moment can he spend on them'.

### 3.3.2  Moving Beyond Bureaucratic Use of Officious and Intrusive Questionnaires

On the other hand, it is clear that Kafka is not an unqualified exponent of bureaucratic data-gathering methods across the board. This can be seen from his interchange with Brod who, while Kafka was resident at the *Tatranskéf Matliary* sanitorium in June 2021,[43] sent him an 'official questionnaire' inquiring after his health 'to be completed and submitted as soon as possible', in what Renier Stach describes as 'a joke between civil servants'.[44] (Brod started worked at the Post Office around the same time that Kafka started at the Institute.) Kafka duly completed and returned the questionnaire, but obliquely responded to Brod's question on 'objective results of lung examination' obliquely with 'doctor's secret: supposedly favourable'.[45] (It was a response which perhaps gave more insight than the question deserved: *viz* that his doctor was reluctant to tell him the true state of his health.)

A similarly sceptical tone is evident in Kafka's story 'Investigations of a Dog' (*Forschungen eines Hundes*),[46] completed a year after the 'official questionnaire' incident, and in the same year as *The Castle*. In this intriguing story, the narrator, reflecting on his inquiry into the true nature of dogs, talks of his 'lack of scientific

---

[40] Ibid. p. 85.

[41] Ibid, p. 84.

[42] Ibid. pp. 82, 85.

[43] Stach (2013), pp. 189–90, 252.

[44] Ibid, p. 256. The questionnaire with Kafka's answers can be found in Kafka (1902–1924), p. 338.

[45] See Stach 2013, 2016, p. 254.

[46] Kafka (1922b).

ability, poor capacity for abstract thought, worse memory, and above all my inability to keep a scientific goal always before me'.[47] Yet, he concludes, his inability is underpinned by 'an instinct, and not a bad instinct at that':[48]

> This was the instinct that – perhaps out of regard for science, but a different sort of science from that practiced today, an ultimate science – has led me to esteem freedom more highly than anything else. Freedom! Freedom as it is on offer to us today is a wretched weed. But it's freedom of a kind, something to possess.[49]

There have been many speculations about the meaning and significance of this story – for instance, that it is a 'mostly tiresome' exercise in tail-chasing,[50] a reflection on 'the self-undermining search for truth, problematic aspects of science, the question of progress',[51] a comment on 'a markedly depleted technical sort of life, beset with imperatives and hierarchies and limitations'.[52] But we can equally understand it as more literally a reflection on the scientific methods of inquiry as 'practiced today' along with a veiled proposal for a 'different sort of science'. Reading Kafka's octavo notebooks from around this period, where he emphasises 'contemplation' ('*Kontemplation*') as adding to 'activity' ('*Tätigkeit*') in discerning 'the truth' ('*Wahrheit*'),[53] we have a sense that the 'different sort' of science he refers to above is one that deploys imagination, sympathy and a degree of self-searching alongside observation. Thus, while Benjamin suggests that Kafka was focussed on constructing a 'complementary world', without any awareness of 'what surrounded him',[54] I suggest that what Kafka points to here is a technique of looking within for insight into the world around.[55]

We arguably see this too in the last unfinished sentence of *The Castle*, a novel that is essentially about 'truth-seeking'.[56] Here K, the would-be bureaucrat, put aside his scientific investigations in response to an old woman of the village (the coachman Gerstäcker's mother) who 'held a trembling hand out to K. and made him sit down beside her, she spoke with an effort, it was an effort to understand her, but what she said'.[57] By this point, when K has exhausted his efforts to find out his status and right to stay in the village through his endless questions, he stands in hope of being granted knowledge freely as a member of the community.

---

[47] Ibid, p. 188.

[48] Ibid.

[49] Ibid, p. 189.

[50] McNamara (2017).

[51] Williams (2007), n 20, quoting Henel (1967), p. 283.

[52] Hofmann in Kafka (1922b), foreword, xv.

[53] Kafka (1918), pp. 117.

[54] Benjamin (1938), p. 143.

[55] Cf Fickert (1993) pp. 195–6.

[56] Corngold 2004, p. 73.

[57] Kafka (1922a), p. 280.

### 3.3.3   New Rights and Obligations to Address Current Social Problems

The last set of examples concern Kafka's vision of law and its conception of rights. Of course, most of Kafka's writings about law offer deep critiques – for instance, his early parable 'Before the Law' (*'Vor dem Gesetz'*), where the law seems infinitely remote and unavailing to the 'man from the country', who becomes trapped in his search for access and meaning,[58] later republished in his dystopian novel *The Trial* (*Der Process*).[59] But at times we can see that he was also interested in the ways that law might be deployed more positively in aid of individual and social rights. One example is the fragment that Brod includes in his biography detailing Kafka's drafting of a utopian scheme for a 'guild' of workers without property.[60] The scheme appears under the title 'The Community of Workers without Property' (*'Die Besitzlose Arbeiterschaft'*) in Kafka's fourth octavo notebook from 1918,[61] and dates to around March of that year.[62] Its list of ideal workers' rights and obligations may have been inspired by political events (the Russian revolution of 1917, political unrest in Germany in the leadup to the November revolution of 1918) but draws as well on Kafka's experience in engaging with workers through his work at the Institute. The list shows Kafka's creativity in devising novel 'rights' and 'obligations' geared to contemporary social purpose, including rights to maximum working-time (6 h or 4–5 h for manual work), to be looked after in sickness and old age in state-run hospitals and institutions, to form a 'works council' (*'Arbeitssrates fügen'*) negotiating under the authority of the Government, and with working life treated as a matter of 'trust' and 'conscience' rather than reverting to the 'law-courts'.[63]

Kafka returned to briefly addresses the theme of the ideal function of law and its institutions in his later essay 'On the Matter of Our Laws' (*Zur frage der gesetze*), where he argues directly that laws should be for the benefit of 'the people' they ostensibly serves, rather than treated as the 'secret' resource skewed in the interests of 'the nobles who govern us'.[64] Indeed, the one 'bright spot' in our current existence, he concludes, is that that 'one day a time will come when tradition and its study will breathe a sigh of relief and reach a conclusion when everything will have been made clear – that the law is the property of the people – and then the nobility will disappear'.[65] Could he be hoping for the same those legal experts on matters of bureaucratic knowledge– such as Bürgel in *The Castle*? Certainly, that would be the

---

[58] Kafka (1915a).

[59] Kafka (1915b).

[60] Brod (1937), pp. 68–9.

[61] Kafka (1918), pp. 126–127.

[62] See Fenves (2011), p. 107.

[63] Kafka (1918), pp. 119–120.

[64] Kafka (1920), pp. 115–117.

[65] Ibid, pp. 116–117.

ultimate freedom for bureaucracy's subjects, to be free of the experts who rely on their interpretations of law's 'traditions' to govern bureaucratic subjects – and to have law designed and practiced to serve their needs and dignities, framing and supporting their rights. The 'rights' that K asks for and does not receive at least from the authorities as a bureaucratic subject in *The Castle*.

## 3.4 Revaluing Kafka in the Search for Data Rights

Revaluing Kafka's story of K and the villagers in *The Castle* in 1944, Arendt posits that 'his behavior teaches them that human rights may be worth fighting for, that the rule of the Castle is not divine law and, consequently, can be attacked'.[66] Indeed, as Brod elaborates in his biography of Kafka, his concern with rights long predated this bureaucratic novel: although he never took an active part in political movements 'his reflective interest was claimed by any efforts that aimed at improving the lot of man'.[67] At the same time, I have argued in this chapter, he had his own ideas about how rights should be framed for the benefit of the people.

Thus we can imagine what Kafka's interest might have been in the United Nations project of framing universal human rights in the aftermath of the second world war, a war in which so many of his family, friends and community perished, became destitute, lost their identities as citizens along with their rights.[68] He might also pay attention to the rather limited way in which the Declaration's civil and political rights were shaped, in contrast to its more radical cataloguing of social rights pushed for by Soviet States but also supported by 'serious 1940s socialist thinkers' like the Canadian John Humphrey, René Cassin from France, Hernan Santa Cruz from Chile, and others involved in the Declaration.[69] Unlike Arendt the scholar-refugee, and Benjamin the unique intellectual, bureaucracy was Kafka's world, giving him a unique insight into the kinds of novel rights that might assist in 'improving the lot of man' in the twentieth century.[70] We have already seen, from Kafka's utopian scheme for 'The Brotherhood for Poor Workers' complete with its list of workmen's rights – including on maximum hours of work, care in illness, and the allocation of work and the role for a works council, Kafka's ability to think constructively in imagining new rights fit for his time. Compare here Kafka's catalogue of workers' rights, framed in the same year as the German Revolution at the end of the first world war, with the Weimar Constitution's catalogue of rights to work, including provision for works councils and trade unions, and to social

---

[66] Arendt (1944), p. 73.

[67] Brod 1937, pp. 68–9.

[68] See Arendt (1949).

[69] Morsink (2021), p. 146.

[70] Brod (1937), p. 68.

'insurance'.[71] and the Universal Declaration's rights 'to work, to free choice of employment, to just and favourable conditions of work and to protection against unemployment' (albeit not to be represented through works councils or trade unions),[72] and 'to security in the event of unemployment, sickness, disability, widowhood, old age or other lack of livelihood in circumstances beyond his control'.[73] It is remarkable how farsighted Kafka's views on workers' rights was as he conceived them in 1918. Why did Kafka not do apply the same prescience to the framing of novel data rights, beyond K's asking for 'my rights' in the face of the bureaucratic machinations of *The Castle*?

Perhaps the answer is that any idea of formulating data rights in the fully modern sense of rights to control the processing of personal information under bureaucracy was still barely on the horizon in 1918. It may well be argued that the participatory self-governing model of the works committee, or works council, provides an interesting prefiguring of such rights. But for the time being they are little more than hinted at by Kafka, or, for that matter, by the framers of the Weimar Constitution, who are more focussed on catering to the political, economic and social needs of soldiers, sailors and workers who fomented the November Revolution while maintaining significant scope for public order to be maintained (including a power to set aside rights in the interests of public order under the notorious art 48, a power later exploited by Hitler in his first moves towards totalitarianism in 1933).[74] And with Weber as one of those consulted in its drafting, it was no doubt difficult to move beyond his theory of rational bureaucracy – even if the Constitution's drafters felt the need to specify that 'public officials are servants of the whole community, and not of a party'.[75] Instead, what the Weimar Constitution comes up with is a sketchy array of rights regarding inviolability of the home, inviolability of secrecy of letters, telegraph, and telephone communications (catering to an extent to the privacy of private life), along with freedom of speech and communication.[76] In the Universal Declaration these rights become transposed into rights of privacy, home and correspondence in art 12, and freedom of thought, opinion and expression in arts 18 and 19, including 'rights to receive and impart information and ideas through any media'.[77] Arts 8 through 10 of the European Convention on Human Rights, agreed 2 years later in the Council of Europe,[78] are expressed in similar terms to these provisions of the Universal Declaration. However, art 1 of the Universal Declaration, declaring that 'human beings are born free and equal in dignity and rights',[79] is

---

[71] Weimar Constitution (Constitution of the German Reich) (1919), arts 157–165.

[72] Universal Declaration of Human Rights, art 23(1).

[73] Ibid, art 25(1).

[74] See generally Stolleis, (2004) ch 3, 45–105; Grégoire (2022).

[75] Weimar Constitution, art 130.

[76] Ibid, arts 115–118.

[77] Universal Declarations (1948), arts 12, 18–19.

[78] European Convention (1950), arts 8–10.

[79] Universal Declaration, art 1. See also Preamble, first and fifth recitals.

without any immediate parallel in the European Convention, being an instrument more focussed on practically 'secur[ing] ... rights and freedoms'.[80] Moreover, a proposed right to 'development of the human personality' was narrowly rejected in favour of a statement of 'the economic, social and cultural rights indispensable for [a person's] dignity and the free development of his personality' in art 22 of the Universal Declaration,[81] a provision explicitly geared to 'social security' (although perhaps better seen as about social justice).[82] This provision, again, has no parallel in the European Convention.[83]

By contrast, the Basic Law of the Federal Republic of Germany (*Grundgesetz*) *of 23 May 1949*, the year after the Universal Declaration (and a year before the European Convention), includes rights to dignity and free development of personality in arts 1 and 2.[84] These rights, serve as immutable foundational rights in this distinctly modern post-war human rights text.[85] While sponsored by the western allied countries in particular the United States as a guard against a repeat of the atrocities of the Nazi period, they also had support from German quarters – including from the head of the 'Committee on Basic Questions' ('*Abteilung für Grundsatzfragen*'), Professor Hermann von Mangoldt, who argued that, after 'a time of continuous oppression and severe disregard for human dignity', Germany had to embrace the 'freedom of the individual'.[86] They are rights that surely Kafka would have approved of given his preoccupations with humanness and his value he ascribes to freedom, 'more highly than anything else'. In the German Census Act case of 1983,[87] they became the basis for the identification of a right to 'informational self-determination' ('*informationelle Selbstbestimmung*') by the Constitutional Court (*Bundesverfassungsgericht*) – framed as a right protecting the individual from 'the unlimited collection, storage, use, and transmission of personal data as a condition for free personality'.[88] The right to informational self-determination finds a parallel in the art 8 right to data protection in the European Union's Charter of Fundamental Rights of 2000 (part of the constitutional law of the European Union by virtue of the Lisbon Treaty of 2007)[89] – stating that '[e]veryone has the right to the protection of personal data concerning him or her ...'.[90] Art 8, with its statement of data rights, in turn forms a groundwork of the EU's General

---

[80] See European Convention, art 1.

[81] Basic Law (1949).

[82] See Morsink (2021), pp. 43–44, 143.

[83] But cf. Council of Europe (1961) art 14.

[84] See Kommers and Miller (2012), pp. 44–5.

[85] Ibid, p. 44.

[86] Spevack (1997), p. 427, citing Von Mangoldt (1949), pp. 261–263.

[87] Census Act Case (1983) in Kommers and Miller, 408–411.

[88] Ibid, p. 410.

[89] EU Treaty of Lisbon (2007).

[90] EU Charter (2000), art 8.

Data Protection Regulation in 2016.[91] At the same time, though, the GDPR also comes on the back of a post-war tradition of data protection rules in Europe that can be seen as quite Weberian, spelling out rule according to rules constraining the bureaucrat's rule by knowledge in distinctly bureaucratic 'rule of law' terms.[92] As data rights scholars have pointed out,[93] there is a tension between the rule-bound orientation of the GDPR as a data protection instrument and the rights orientation of its underpinning in the Charter and its art 8 in particular. But the rights dimension is becoming more explicit and dominant in current data protection jurisprudence. And, in the exercise of creatively interpreting and applying data protection standards in our current bureaucratised societies, we could benefit from looking to Kafka's call for 'my rights' in his bureaucratic novel of the 1920s.

# References

Arendt H (1944) Franz Kafka: a revaluation, 11 Partisan Review. In: Arendt H 1994) Hannah Arendt: Essays in understanding, 1930–1954 (ed Kohn J). Harcourt Brace, New York, pp 69–80

Arendt H (1949) 'The rights of man': what are they? Mod Rev 3(1):24–36

Benjamin W (1934), Franz Kafka on the tenth anniversary of his death. In: Benjamin W (1969), Illuminations (trans: Zohn H, ed and intro Arendt H). Schocken, New York, pp 111–140

Benjamin W (1938), Some reflections on Kafka. In: Benjamin W (1969), Illuminations (trans: Zohn H, ed and intro Arendt H). Schocken, New York, pp 141–145

Brod M (1937), Franz Kafka: eine biographie. Heinrich Mercy Sohn, Prague. In Brod M (1947) Franz Kafka: a biography (trans: G Humphreys Roberts). Secker & Warburg, London

Census Act Case (1983) 65 BVerfGE 1. In: Kommers D and Miller RA (2012) The constitutional jurisprudence of the federal republic of Germany, 3rd edn. Duke University Press, Chapel Hill, pp 408–411 (extract)

Clifford D (2023) Data protection law and emotion. Oxford University Press, Oxford

Constitution of the German Reich (Die Verfassung des Deutschen Reichs) (1919) (Office of US Chief of Counsel, trans of document 2050-PS)

Corngold S (2004) Franz Kafka: the radical modernist. In: Bartram G (ed) The Cambridge companion to the modern German novel. Cambridge University Press, Cambridge, pp 62–75

Council of Europe (1950) European Convention for the Protection of Human Rights and Fundamental Freedoms, as amended by Protocols No 11 and 14. ETS 5, Rome

Council of Europe (1961) European Social Charter. ETS No 035, Turin

de Hert P, Gutwirth S (2009) Data protection in the case law of Strasbourg and Luxemburg: constitutionalisation in action. In: Gutwirth S, Poullet Y, de Hert P, Terwangne C, Nouwt S (eds) Reinventing data protection? Springer, Dordrecht

Dickens C (1850) The personal history, adventures, experience and observation of David Copperfield the younger of Blunderstone Rookery. In: Dickens C (2000) David Copperfield (intro Gavin AE). Wordsworth, Hertfordshire

Duttlinger C (2017) Introduction. In: Duttlinger C (ed) Franz Kafka in context. Cambridge University Press, Cambridge, pp 1–5

European Union (2000) Charter of Fundamental Rights of the European Union, *2000*/C 364/01

---

[91] *Regulation* (EU) 2016/679.

[92] See de Hert and Gutwirth (2009), p. 9.

[93] See generally Clifford (2023).

European Union (2007) Treaty of Lisbon amending the Treaty on European Union and the Treaty Establishing the European Community, 2007/C 306/01

Federal Republic of Germany (1949, May 23) Basic law for the Federal Republic of Germany (Grundgesetz). Germany

Fenves P (2011) 'Workforce without possessions': Kafka, 'social justice', and the word religion. In: Kordela AK, Vardoulakis D (eds) Freedom and confinement in modernity: Kafka's cages. Palgrave Macmillan, New York, pp 107–126

Fickert K (1993) Kafka's search for truth in 'forschungen eines hundes'. Monatshefte 85(2):189–197

Grégoire G (2022) The economic constitution under Weimar: doctrinal controversies and ideological struggles. In: Grégoire G, Miny X (eds) The idea of economic constitution in Europe: genealogy and overview. Brill Nijhoff, Leiden, pp 53–93

Hamilton JT (2023) France/Kafka: an author in theory. Bloomsbury Academic, London

Heide L (2009) Punched-card systems and the early information explosion, 1880–1945. Johns Hopkins University Press, Baltimore

Henel I (1967) Die deutbarkeit von Kafkas werken. Zeitschrift für Deutsche Philologie 86:250–266

Jørgensen T (2012) Weber and Kafka: the rational and the enigmatic bureaucracy. Public Admin 90(1):194–210

Kafka F (1902–1924) Briefe: In Kafka F Briefe (1958) (ed Brod M). Schocken, New York

Kafka F (1909–1917) Amtliche schriften. In: Kafka F (2009) Franz Kafka: the office writings (ed Greenberg J, Corngold S, Wagner B, trans: Patton E, Hein R). Princeton University Press, Princeton

Kafka F (1915a) Vor dem gesetz (Before the law). In: Kafka F (1917) Ein landarzt; kleine erzählungen. Kurt Wolff, München; (1945), pp 49–56

Kafka F (1915b), Der process (The trial). In: Kafka (1925) Der process (ed Brod M). Verlag Die Schmiede, Berlin

Kafka F (1918) Das vierte oktavheft (The fourth octavo notebook). In: Kafka F (1953) Hochzeitsvorbereitungen auf dem lande und andere prosa aus dem nachlass (ed Brod M). Schocken, New York, pp 106–131

Kafka F (1920) Zur frage der gesetze (On the matter of our laws), In: Kafka F (2017) Investigations of a dog, and other creatures (trans: Hofmann M). New Directions, New York, pp 115–117

Kafka F (1922a) Das schloß. In: Kafka (1997) The castle (trans: Underwood JA, from Kafka F (1982)) Das schloß (Pasley M herausgegeben), vol 1. Fischer, Frankfurt am M. Penguin, London

Kafka F (1922b) Forschungen eines hundes (Investigations of a dog). In Kafka F (2017) Investigations of a dog, and other creatures (trans: Hofmann M). New Directions, New York, pp 146–189

Kommers D, Miller RA (2012) The constitutional jurisprudence of the Federal Republic of Germany, 3rd edn. Duke University Press, Chapel Hill

Litowitz D (2011) Max Weber and Franz Kafka: a shared vision of modern law. Law Cult Humanit 7(1):48–65

McNamara NS (2017) Midnight madness: Franz Kafka's 'Investigations of a dog: and other creatures'. Los Angeles Review of Books

Melville H (1853) Bartleby, the scrivener: a story of Wall-Street. In: Melville H (2007) Bartleby the scrivener (McGrath P foreword). Hersperus, London

Morsink J (2021) Article by article: the universal declaration of human rights for a new generation. University of Pennsylvania Press, Philadelphia

Regulation (EU) 2016/679 of the *European* Parliament and of the Council of 27 April 2016 on the *protection* of natural persons with regard to the processing and on the free movement of such data, and repealing Directive 95/46/EC (GDPR)

Spevack E (1997) American pressures on the German constitutional tradition: basic rights in the west German constitution of 1949. Int J Polit Cult Soc 10(3):411–436

Stach R (2013) Kafka: the years of insight (trans: Frisch S). Princeton University Press, Princeton

Stach R (2016) Is that Kafka? 99 finds (Is das Kafka? 99 fundstücke) (trans: Beals K). New Directions, New York

Stolleis M (2004) A *history* of public law in *Germany* 1914–1945 (trans: Dunlap T). Oxford University Press, Oxford

United Nations General Assembly (1948, December 10) Universal Declaration of Human Rights. Res 217 A(III)

Verne J (1863) Paris au XXe siècle. In: Verne J (1996) Paris in the twentieth century (trans: Howard R, intro Weber E). Random House, New York

Vismann C (2000) Atken. medientechnik und recht. In: Vismann C (2008) Files: law and media technology (trans: Winthrop-Young G). Stanford University Press, Stanford

von Mangoldt H (1949) Grundrechte und grundsatzfragen des Bonner Grundgesetzes. Archiv des öffentlichen Rechts 75(36/3):273–290

Wagner B (2006) Insuring Nietzsche: Kafka's files. New German Critique 33(99):83–119

Warner BE (2001) John Stuart Mill's theory of bureaucracy within representative government: balancing competence and participation. Public Admin Rev 61(4):403–413

Weber A (1910) Der beamte. In: Harrington A (2007) Alfred Weber's essay 'the civil servant' and Kafka's 'in the penal colony': the evidence of an influence. Hist Hum Sci 20(3):21–63

Weber M (1917) Wissenschaft als beruf. In Weber M (1958) Science as a vocation. Daedalus 87(1): 111–134

Weber M (1920) Wirtschaft und gesellschaft. In Weber M (2019) Economy and society: a new translation (ed and trans: Tribe K). Harvard University Press, Cambridge

Williams E (2007) Of cinema, food, and desire: Franz Kafka's 'investigations of a dog. Coll Lit 34(4):92–124

# Chapter 4
# Resisting Cinematographic Mechanism

**Abstract** This chapter turns to the challenges posed for human identity by an increasingly pervasive and mechanised early twentieth century arts and entertainment industry dedicated to recording and replaying fictionalised accounts of human life stories for public enlightenment and entertainment. Henri Bergson's vitalist arguments for individual creative evolution as opposed to 'cinematic mechanism' in *Creative Evolution* (*L'Évolution créatrice*) inspired a generation captivated by the Bergsonian idea of 'creativity, change and freedom' – including plaintiffs and judges in diverse legal cases of the 1920s and 1930s. Their reasoning takes on a new significance in developing data rights around erasure/forgetting and rectification in our current highly mechanised and networked world which challenges forgetting and problematises distinctions between true and false, free and determined.

**Keywords** Identity · Bergson · Cinematographic mechanism · Right to erasure · Right to be forgotten · Right to rectification · Right not to be subject to automated decision-making

## 4.1 Introduction

To quote Henri Bergson at the dawn of the twentieth century, '[w]herever anything lives, there is, open somewhere, a register in which time is being inscribed'.[1] At the same time, the human subjects of inscription, each engaged in a process of creative evolution under which their personality 'shoots, grows, and ripens without ceasing',[2] may have their own ideas as to how (or if) they should be recorded. The situation creates the possibility of numerous sites of contestation in an age marked, among other things, by an increasingly pervasive and mechanised modern arts and entertainment industry dedicated to recording and replaying fictionalised accounts of

---

[1] Bergson (1907), p 17.

[2] Ibid, p. 6.

M. Richardson, *The Right to Privacy 1914–1948*, SpringerBriefs in Law, https://doi.org/10.1007/978-981-99-4498-9_4

human life stories for public enlightenment and entertainment.[3] On the one hand, per Michel Foucault, there is the agency, organisation or individual with official status as controller of the record and its 'order[ed] ... knowledge'.[4] On the other hand, there are the Foucauldian 'subjugated' 'popular knowledges' and 'counter memories' of those who may be marginalised and excluded in society,[5] which 'in union' with ordered knowledge may be brought together to establish a more complex 'genealogy' of historical struggles. Finally (possibly overlapping with the second category), there are the individual human subjects of knowledge who risk losing control over their identities in the maelstrom of knowledge.

In this chapter, I consider how plaintiffs and judges in legal cases of the 1920s and 1930s looked for ways to address this problem, turning to an array of rights and laws around *droit l'auteur*, privacy, reputation and even 'happiness' to support the efforts of individuals (engaged in processes of creative evolution) to tell their own stories. I argue that their reasoning takes on a new significance in developing data rights around erasure/forgetting and rectification in our current highly mechanised and networked world which challenges forgetting and problematises distinctions between true and false, free and determined.

## 4.2   Bergson and Bergsonism

There were earlier strains of vitalist thinking prior to Bergson's appearance eg, the leading English liberal-utilitarian philosopher John Stuart Mill who in *On Liberty* in 1859 argued famously that '[h]uman nature is not a machine to be built after a model, and set to do exactly the work prescribed for it, but a tree, which requires to grow and develop itself on all sides, according to the tendency of the inward forces which make it a living thing';[6] and the American pragmatist (and Bergson's great friend and admirer) William James who in his 'Remarks on Spencer's Definition of Mind as Correspondence' in 1878 offered the insight that '[t]he knower is an actor, and co-efficient of the truth on one side, whilst on the other he registers the truth which he helps to create'.[7] But as Hannah Arendt points out in her Gifford lectures on 'The Life of the Mind', delivered at the University of Aberdeen in 1972–1974, Bergson was more radical in his understanding and explaining of the past as a 'mode of potentiality in advance of its own actualisation'.[8] Indeed, as a leading figure of the modernist *avant garde*, Bergson was clearly well ahead of his time in his

---

[3] See Hobsbawm (1994), ch 6.

[4] Foucault (1976), p. 83.

[5] Ibid, pp. 82–3.

[6] Mill (1859), p. 188.

[7] James (1878), p. 17.

[8] Arendt (1978), p. 31.

imagination of the creative impulse (*'élan vital'*) involved in the shaping of an individual's present and future way of being.

In Bergson's Gifford lectures, on 'the problem of personality', delivered in 1914 at the University of Edinburgh (the second series was abandoned with the advent of war), Bergson draws on and elaborates his earlier arguments in *Creative Evolution* in 1907 – observing that, still in 1914, 'we are faced by the difficulty of finding a place for personality, that is to say, of admitting real individualities possessing an effective independence, each of which would constitute a little world in the bosom of the great world'.[9] In *Creative Evolution* he puts this down to the mechanism of modern society, bolstered by the philosophical determinism of Victorian philosopher Herbert Spencer and his ilk. Spencer's scientific doctrine bearing the name of 'social evolution', Bergson says, 'dealt neither with becoming nor with evolution'.[10] Rather, his 'illusion' is that, if he takes what is already known, breaks it up and scatters it into 'fragments', then reintegrates the fragments, he displays its 'genesis': whereas in truth he gives barely an imitation of 'the more complex effects', 'neither ... [has he] retraced the genesis, and 'the addition of evolved to evolved' bears 'no resemblance ... to the movement of evolution'.[11] As such, Spencer's and the modern scientific method, as well as much 'ordinary knowledge',[12] operates on a mode that Bergson labels as 'cinematographic mechanism' (*'mécanisme cinématographique'*), capturing neatly its essential constructed, or manufactured, character:

> [In order that] pictures may be animated, there must be movement somewhere. The movement does indeed exist here; it is in the apparatus. It is because the film of the cinematograph unrolls, bringing in turn the different photographs of the scene to continue each other, that each actor of the scene recovers his mobility; he strings all his successive attitudes on the invisible movement of the film. The process then consists in extracting from all the movements peculiar to all the figures an impersonal movement abstract and simple, *movement in general*, so to speak: we put this into the apparatus, and we reconstitute the individuality of each particular movement by combining this nameless movement with the personal attitudes. Such is the contrivance of the cinematograph [*Tel est l'artifice du cinématographique*].[13]

Bergson was writing at an early point of cinema's development as a mimetic apparatus, which (as his later supporter and defender Gilles Deleuze points out) preceded its more openly creative uses in later iterations.[14] He acknowledge that he had only seen cinema at its very beginning, never to return to observe its development.[15] Nevertheless, his enduring insight is that there may still be a fundamental failure to apply an 'intelligent' approach to what is going on here, *viz* to appreciate 'the inser-

---

[9] Bergson (1914).

[10] Bergson (1907), p. 385.

[11] Ibid.

[12] Ibid, p. 323.

[13] Bergson (1907), pp. 322–323.

[14] See Deleuze (1983), (1985).

[15] See Georges-Michel (1914).

tion of our will into the reality'.[16] Indeed, his insight can be taken further to argue that any attempt to reduce personality to a series of images (or, we might say today, data points), while presenting it as something that captures the process of free human evolution, risks the same problem. Moreover, in the end, the problem is not just one of illusion. For the basic tenet of the mechanistic approach is that human personality can in fact, over time, be subjected to mechanism's laws of 'similarity' and 'repetition'.[17] As Bergson puts it, we can submit to mechanism, but in the process we find ourselves forced into a regime of 'mechanical adjustment': in adapting to the 'ready-made' we are diminished in personality.[18]

Bergson, or perhaps to be more precise Bergsonism,[19] inspired a generation of modern artists, who steered away from pseudo-realistic representations of the past and in favour of imaginative accounts of the present and future.[20] His influence was obvious on the futurists who in their 'Manifesto of Futurism' issued in 1909 called for speed and destruction and revival,[21] the Dadaists, cubists and fauvists bent on taking existing objects and images and reconfiguring them to produce a wholly new effect,[22] and the surrealists who – rather perversely – established a 'Bureau for Surrealist Research' in Paris in 1924, with the aim of 'gather[ing] all the information possible related to forms that might express the unconscious activity of the mind', while ending up presenting bizarrely distorted versions of these activities.[23] He also inspired a broader generation of poets, philosophers and intellectuals who interpreted and extended his ideas about vitalism versus mechanism in highly diverse ways. Some of these attended his crowded lectures at the Collège de France, along with large numbers of lay auditors (as Charles Péguy wrote in 1902, 'everyone was there').[24] Likewise, in England when Bergson appeared at the University of London in October 1911, lecturing on '*la nature de l'ame*', a 'very large audience' assembled, as reported in *The Times*.[25] The *Illustrated London News* had already warned that the University might expect a 'fashionable' audience, based on the French experience.[26] In New York he reportedly stopped traffic on Broadway when he arrived to give lectures at Columbia University on '"*spiritualite" et liberte*' the year before his Gifford lectures in Edinburgh.[27] But as Emily Herring reports, it was

---

[16] Bergson (1907), p. 323.

[17] Ibid, p. 47.

[18] Ibid, p 61.

[19] Deleuze (1983), p. xiv.

[20] See generally Antliff (1993).

[21] Marinetti (1909), pp. 49–53.

[22] Metzinger (1911), Duchamp (1958) quoted in Kolb (2019), p. 87.

[23] See Durozoi (2002), pp. 63–64.

[24] Péguy (1902) quoted in Bistis (1996), p. 391.

[25] The Times (1911).

[26] Illustrated London News (1911).

[27] See McGrath (2013).

**Fig. 4.1** Philosophy as Fashionable as a Wedding, drawn by René Lelong, Illustrated London News, June 3, 1911, p. 849 (detail). (Public domain, courtesy State Library Victoria, Melbourne)

women especially who found inspiration in his advocacy for 'creativity, change and freedom', speaking to their concerns (Fig. 4.1).[28]

## 4.3  Bergsonism in Legal Action

Finally, Bergsonism seems to have had its effect on the law, albeit this was patchy and incomplete during his lifetime. We might have expected to see this in the French *droit à l'image*, a law devised to protect 'the external visible form' of the human 'physiognomy … [which] reflects the soul and distinguishes the man from his fellow-man'.[29] As Henri Fougerol notes in his early study, titled *La Figure Humaine et le Droit* (The Human Face and the Law), cinema and photography had long been a catalyst for legal formulation of rights against unwanted recording of the image.[30] But in the cases that Fougerol considers, being mainly cases of the second half of the nineteenth century and early twentieth century, the courts treat the image as revealing something essential about the person – per Fougerol, offering a window

---

[28] Herring (2019).

[29] Fougerol (1913), p. 4.

[30] Ibid, pp. 7–9.

into the individual's 'soul'.[31] Even the famous *Dumas* case of 1867,[32] where the Paris court concluded that the author Alexandre Dumas should be able to withdraw consent to publication of photographs which showed him in a scandalous associa- tion with young Texan actress Adah Menken, was reasoned on the basis that his private life must be 'walled' off (*'murée'*) and shielded from public opinion.[33] That reasoning fits neatly with the idea of privacy as a right not to be subject to the public gaze, as talked about in earlier chapters in this book (in particular Chap. 2). But if we take a more Bergsonian line, the argument should rather be one of the narrow and artificial exercise of the camera's efforts to capture and memorialise the photo- graphic subject without reflecting the subject's changing life and identity over time.

By contrast, when it came to the less well-known moral right of withdrawal (*le droit de repentir ou de retrait*) of an author or artist under French law, treated as part of *droit d'auteur* in *Camoin c Carco* in 1927,[34] a more Bergsonian style of reasoning emerges. No doubt this had much to do with the way the case was presented by the plaintiff, Charles Camoin, former fauvist artist aligned with Henri Matisse (an admirer of Bergson), and a veteran of the first world war's camouflage unit which had achieved some notoriety for its deployment of modern artistic techniques to cleverly obscure and protect tanks, weapons, observation posts and soldiers from enemy attack. During the war, the camoufleurs formed a 'society' of 'warrior artists, cubists, and "roundist", futurists even pompiers and jokers',[35] working under the guidance of Parisian portrait painter Lucien-Victor Guirand de Scévola.[36] In this case, however, Camoin's purpose seemed to be one of public objection to the sub- merging of his identity through the collective action of those seeking to exercised control over his artistic efforts, and reassertion of his sovereignty over the presenta- tion – or not – of the outputs of his creative labour.[37]

The case was instituted after Camoin found that 60 pictures ripped up by him (being deemed unsatisfactory) and left for rubbish behind his studio in Montmartre in the summer of 1914, shortly before he left for the battlefield – at which point he 'proceeded to forget about them',[38] had been recovered by a ragpicker with the frag- ments sold on. A number of these ended up with the defendant the author Francis Carco who put them up for sale after the war. Camoin initiated legal proceedings and, as the case was reported in the *New York Times,* once the case was lodged to recover his pictures, plus damages, 'all the present owners have been ordered to appear in court to show cause why they should not give them up'.[39] The *Tribunal*

---

[31] Cf Wagner (1970), p. 1.

[32] *Dumas c Liébert*, Cour D'Appel de Paris, 25 May 1867, S 1868.2.41.

[33] Ibid, p 42. And see Wagner, pp. 9–10.

[34] *Camoin c Carco*, Trib Civile la Seine, 15 November 1927, DP 1928.2.89. Judgment confirmed *Carco c Camoin*, Cour D'Appel de Paris, 6 March 1931, DP 1931.2.88.

[35] André Mare (1916), pp. 1–2, as quoted in Kahn (1984) p. 39.

[36] See generally Kahn, ch 2.

[37] Cf Syed (2016), p. 514.

[38] *New York Times* (1926), p. 4.

[39] Ibid.

*Civile la Seine* in a radical move upheld Camoin's claim, holding that not only had the fragments of his destroyed artworks been recovered against Camoin's will and then presented under his signature, again against his will, but those in possession of the fragments embarked upon the task 'familiar to all artists' of bringing together the scattered fragments, eliminating the appearance of the tears, and even 'complet[ing] work where parts were missing', while gluing together others.[40] In short, the court concluded (here adopting a distinctly Bergsonian tone):

> in accomplishing the work of reconstitution of these paintings, they have substituted themselves for the artist without his knowledge and against his free will, they have redone the artist's creation, that which was the expression of the artist's thought, personality, talent, art, and one could say, in terms of philosophy, the artist's very individuality.[41]

However, it was an unusual Californian 'privacy' case that transposed Bergsonian ideas of cinematic mechanism into the field of cinema specifically, *viz* the 1931 case of *Melvin v Reid*.[42] The case was launched in response to Hollywood silent film melodrama *The Red Kimona* (or *The Red Kimono* according to the advertising posters and newspaper advertisements),[43] which drew on the life story of former prostitute and murder-accused Gabrielle Darley Melvin. This connection is made directly in Dorothy Davenport Reid's opening introductory words to the camera, where she identifies the plaintiff Darley Melvin by name and references newspaper accounts of a notorious murder case from 16 years earlier where Darley Melvin was accused of murdering the man she was hoping to marry (who she claimed had stolen her money to buy a ring for another woman) but was exonerated by the jury. It may be fair to say that Davenport's activism in producing, directing albeit without credit, and introducing this sympathetic account of Darley Melvin's life-history gives valuable expression to the social plight of many marginalised women in the United States in the 1920s.[44] But on Darley Melvin's side, we are confronted with a real person's complicated efforts at self-presentation in the face of the film's determined replaying of details of her earlier life, combined with the overlay of Davenport Reid's interpretations and judgements, ordering the audience's assumed knowledge of her character then and now. This is evident, for instance, in Darley Melvin's argument that she had by the time of the film entered into 'an exemplary, virtuous, honorable and righteous life' as a married woman, thereby assuming 'a place in respectable society', and 'made many friends who were not aware of the incidents of her earlier life' – adding that the film's revelations of the unsavoury events of her earlier life 'caused them to scorn and abandon her and exposed her to obloquy, contempt, and ridicule, causing her grievous mental and physical suffering'.[45]

---

[40] *Camoin c Carco*, p 92 (Trib Civile la Seine).

[41] Ibid.

[42] *Melvin v Reid*, 112 Cal App 285 (Cal Ct App 1931).

[43] Lang (1925).

[44] See Anderson (n.d.).

[45] *Melvin v Reid*, pp. 286–287 (Marks J).

The court in upholding her claim seemed sympathetic to Darley Melvin's argument that the film's presentation of her former life transgressed her ability to reconstitute her identity, with the judge Emerson J Marks drawing on unnamed sociological sources to press the view that:

> One of the major objectives of society as it is now constituted, and of the administration of our penal system, is the rehabilitation of the fallen and the reformation of the criminal. Under these theories of sociology it is our object to lift up and sustain the unfortunate rather than tear him down. Where a person has by his own efforts rehabilitated himself, we, as right-thinking members of society, should permit him to continue in the path of rectitude rather than throw him back into a life of shame or crime.[46]

Yet, despite the language of 'privacy' in the judgment, there is little of what might be called a right to the privacy of a private life subjected to unwanted public exposure, as talked about by Samuel Warren and Louis Brandeis in their 1890 *Harvard Law Review* article (which is also cited in the judgment).[47] Nor does this case fit easily into the category of defamation, focussed on the vindication a person's public reputation, despite its deliberately exaggerated character as a moral tale of redemption. Rather, the judge's statement above about rehabilitation and reformation seems more to emphasise a Bergsonian understanding of the individual' personality as fluid, developing and multidimensional. And although some scholars suggest the court was especially sympathetic to the plaintiff's plight because Darley Melvin was a woman,[48] Marks J's default masculine language seems to belie this in emphasising a person's 'own efforts' in 'rehabilitat[ing] ... himself'. If anything, this language seems to stress the modern man as the quintessential modern individual looking for rehabilitation – in the same way that a decade later modern architects George Nelson and Henry Wright talk about 'individuality' as desired by 'the modern man' as requiring a new architecture geared to 'be[ing] able to meet every requirement of contemporary living',[49] in *Tomorrow's House.*[50] And, if there is a criticism to be made here of Marks J along with Nelson and Wright, it is their deployment of conventionally masculine language at the same time as they call for a new approach to an issue that manifestly affects diverse individuals, women included. For ultimately the court in *Melvin v Reid* also calls for a new approach, albeit in more subtle terms than Nelson and Wright in their manifesto (and one even more ahead of its time in terms of what US courts have been willing to embrace).[51] Thus Marks J notes that the right to happiness in the California constitution may be the best basis for allowing 'a freedom from unnecessary attacks on ... [a person's]

---

[46] Ibid, 291–2.

[47] Warren and Brandeis (1890).

[48] See Allen and Mack (1989), p. 470. Cf Lake (2016), p. 199.

[49] Ibid, p. 9.

[50] Nelson and Wright (1945), pp. 6–7.

[51] Contrast *Sidis v FR Pub. Corporation*, 113 F2d 806 (2d Cir 1940), followed in *Time, Inc v Hill*, 385 US 374 (1967)

character, social standing or reputation',[52] and '[w]hether we call this a right of privacy or give it any other name is immaterial because it is a right guaranteed by our Constitution that must not be ruthlessly and needlessly invaded by others'.[53]

A similarly unusually extended treatment was accorded to the law of defamation in the English case of *Youssoupoff v Metro-Goldwyn-Mayer Pictures, Ltd*,[54] another case involving a Hollywood scandalous biopic in the pre-Code era (before the Hays code introduced a regime of self-censorship).[55] The plaintiff was Princess Irina Youssoupoff, formerly Princess Yusupova of Russia, who following the Russian Revolution moved to Paris with minimal resources and together with her husband Prince Félix established the successful fashion house, *Irfé* with branches in Paris and London until it closed in 1931 in the midst of the Depression. Her complaint concerned MGN's 1932 film *Rasputin the Mad Monk*, (*Rasputin and the Empress* in the United States) which, while claiming to be based on real-life events with some of its characters now dead and others still living, contained a highly fictionalised account of Rasputin's relationship of influence within the household of Emperor Nicholas II and Empress Alexandra before the Revolution – being an account based on a screenplay by left-wing German expressionist writer 'Klabund' (Alfred Henschke), also published as a novel in 1929.[56]

Among the various notorious events depicted in the film (and book) was the death of Rasputin's at the hands of Prince Félix (named Prince Chegodieff in the film) and his co-conspirators in his Moika Canal palace in St Petersburg in December 1916. Prince Félix had given his own accounts of his involvement in the murder. For instance, he apparently told the suffragette Emmeline Pankhurst who was visiting Russia at the time of the Revolution, who in turn repeated it to American journalist Rheta Louise Child Dorr who wrote about it in her 1917 book *Inside the Russian Revolution*.[57] And he discussed it further in his memoir published in 1927.[58] This was presumably the reason he was not a plaintiff in this case. However, the film went well beyond a simple factual account in giving expression to rumours that had been circulating at the time of the murder (noted by Dorr),[59] that a particular motivation for Prince Felix's actions was Rasputin's 'lascivious[ness]' towards Princess Irina (Princess Natasha in the film). Prince Félix countered the film's version in evidence in court, reported in *The Times*, noting that Irina had never met Rasputin and testifying directly that he believed he was 'acting in the service' of his country in carrying out the execution.[60] In her own evidence,

---

[52] *Melvin v Reid*, p 291 (Marks J).

[53] Ibid, p. 292.

[54] *Youssoupoff v Metro-Goldwyn- Mayer Pictures Ltd* (1934) 50 TLR 581 (CA).

[55] See Doherty (1999).

[56] Klabund (1929). See Gilman (1988).

[57] Dorr (1917), pp. 98–102.

[58] Yusupov (1927), ch 3.

[59] Dorr (1917), p. 98.

[60] *The Times* (1934b), p. 4.

Princess Irina stated that her purpose in bringing the proceedings was to 'vindicate' her 'character' (Fig. 4.2).[61]

As there is nothing to suggest that the film had any impact on Princess Irina's reputation in her own circle,[62] it seems the issue was how she would be viewed for posterity by a wider public that was less acquainted with her life history. Evidently the jury thought she had been defamed, with substantial damages awarded in the trial,[63] and upheld on appeal.[64] Even Scrutton LJ, a judge notoriously averse to 'sociological vision',[65] considered that it went without saying that Princess Irina suffered public 'discredit' as a result of her portrayal as raped or seduced by Rasputin in MGN's *The Mad Monk*, a film that had already been viewed by

**Fig. 4.2** Prince Felix Yussupoff, at whose palace on the Moika Canal Rasputin was killed, and his wife, the Grand Duchess Irene Alexandrovna, niece of the late Czar, Boasson and Eggler, St. Petersburg, 1914, in Rheta Louise Child Dorr, *Inside the Russian Revolution* (1917), after p. 92 (detail)

---

[61] *The Times* (1934a), p. 4.

[62] Ibid.

[63] *The Times* (1934c), p. 5.

[64] *Youssoupoff v MGN*, p 584 (Scrutton LJ).

[65] *Place v Searle* [1932] 2 KB 497, pp. 516–517 (Scrutton LJ) contra McCardie J at p. 503.

'an enormous number' of people by the time the case came to court.[66] Indeed, this judge seemed remarkably unconcerned about establishing precisely what the present audience might think about the effects of an imputation of rape or seduction on a woman in the 1930s (beyond making clear it was a question for the jury).[67] Perhaps this was because he appreciated that the impact of the cinematic record was not just for present but for future audiences. As he went on to state, the film was 'so far from the real facts in some cases that one regrets that it was represented at all as being any genuine representation of the facts which had happened'.[68] While Bergson might say that the idea of there being 'any genuine representation' of what happened in any mechanistic retelling is an illusion, it seems this highly practical judge, noted for his refusal to countenance pretence,[69] could at least see the illusion where the cinematic retelling of events is clearly 'far removed' from being a 'genuine representation' of what had occurred.

## 4.4 Towards a Bergsonian Right of Creative Evolution

That these cases, along with their reasoning, were disparate cases of another era may help to explain why little of these ways of thinking appear to have been reflected in the debates leading up to the Universal Declaration of Human Rights in 1948.[70] Instead, we have the binaries of art 12's protection of privacy along with dignity and reputation, on the one hand, and art 19's freedom of opinion and speech on the other,[71] (with the latter treated as 'the highest aspiration of the common people in the Preamble).[72] Freedom of thought in art 17, which might include a freedom to think about oneself, is subsumed under a more general provision about freedom of religion.[73] In the negotiations, René Cassin suggested that that 'freedom of thought had a metaphysical significance', a possible allusion to Bergson, but others at the bargaining table felt that this article was 'intended essentially to protect religious freedom',[74] and that is how it came out. By 1948, it seems, Bergsonism had fallen from favour. It probably did not help that Bergson led the League of Nations' International Commission on Intellectual Cooperation in the 1920s, which not only failed to achieve cooperation but failed to avert a second world war.[75] And it

---

[66] *Youssoupoff v MGN* (1934), pp. 584–585 (Scrutton LJ).

[67] See (critically) Pruitt (2004), p. 445; Mitchell (2015), pp. 91–92.

[68] *Youssoupoff v MGN*, p. 584. See Davis (1988).

[69] Llewellyn (1936), pp. 699–700.

[70] Universal Declaration of Human Rights (1948).

[71] Ibid, art 12; art 19.

[72] Ibid, Preamble, second recital.

[73] Ibid, art 17.

[74] See Morsink (2021), pp. 118–119.

[75] Canales (2005).

probably did not help either that Bergson was dead from the early days of the second world war. His last book, *Two Sources of Morality and Religion* (*Les Deux Sources de la Morale et de la Religion*),[76] where he espoused the creative evolution of an open society embracing all humanity and motivated by a sense of liberty, equality and fraternity (or 'love'), was published in the early 1930s just as Hitler's fascist regime was becoming established in Germany. And, having declined as a notable figure to be designated an 'honorary Aryan' and lined up alongside other Jews in Paris to be registered under the Vichy government in France in the winter of 1940–1941, he suffered the bronchitis that killed him.[77] As Alexandre Lefebvre says, it was '[a] sad end for a man who ... was often reproached for optimism in his philosophy',[78] although Lefebvre also hopefully argues that the spirit of love that Bergson espoused in *Two Sources* should be viewed as an underpinning of modern human rights.

In more recent years, we start to see a more specific hint of Bergsonian freedom in opposition to mechanism in the 1978 French data protection law's general mandate that automated data processing should infringe 'neither human identity, nor the rights of man, nor private life, nor individual or public liberties',[79] and the 2016 General Data Protection Regulation's implementation of the EU Charter's art 8 right to 'the protection of personal data',[80] conceived as a right geared *inter alia* to 'freedom, security and justice and ... to the well-being of natural persons'.[81] Further, the latter's right to rectification and right to erasure (or 'right to be forgotten' – although this is language which surely Bergson would not have approved)[82] are rights which draw on the French data protection law's provisions for rectification, completion, clarification, updating and effacing/deletion (*rectifiées, complétées, clariiées, mises à jour ou effaces*) of the record.[83] Clearly these laws extend to mechanistic modes of memorialisation going well beyond the rather narrow parameters of the GDPR's art 22 right not to be subject to wholly automated decision-making (which also has a parallel in the French data protection law).[84] Already, in the legal cases under these erasure and rectification provisions, we have examples of people seeking to use these rights to move beyond their past lives and embrace a new way of being,[85] or objecting to their way their life histories are being recorded

---

[76] Bergson (1932).

[77] Lefebvre (2018), p. 87.

[78] Ibid, ch 5 and passim.

[79] Loi n° 78–17 (1978), art 1.

[80] EU Charter (2000), art 8.

[81] *Regulation (EU)* 2016/679, recitals 1, 2.

[82] *Ibid*, arts 16, 17.

[83] Loi n° 78–17, art 36.

[84] Regulation (EU) 2016/679, art 22. Cf Loi n° 78–17, arts 2, 3.

[85] Eg *Diana Z c Google*, Tribunal de grande instance de Paris Ordonnance de référé 15 février 2012; *Case C-136/17 GC and Others v Commission nationale de l'informatique et des libertés (CNIL)* (CJEU, Grand Chamber), 24 September 2019.

to begin with,[86] in our highly mechanised and networked world. Likewise, plaintiffs and judges in 'privacy' cases more generally draw on ideas of human flourishing,[87] even if they do not go quite so far as to say that the problem of cinematographic mechanism (which Bergson rightly argued is much about mechanistic thinking as about mechanistic technologies) is the illusion that what is recorded represents the individual person then or in the process of becoming.

# References

Allen AL, Mack E (1989) How privacy got its gender. North Ill Univ Law Rev 10(3):441–478

Anderson ML (n.d.) Dorothy Davenport Reid. Women Film Pioneers Project. https://wfpp.columbia.edu/pioneer/ccp-dorothy-davenport-reid/

Antliff M (1993) Inventing Bergson: cultural politics and the Parisian avant-garde. Princeton University Press, Princeton

Arendt H (1978) The Life of the Mind, vol 2. Harcourt Brace Jovonavoch, New York

Bergson H (1907) L'Évolution créatrice. In: Bergson H (1912) Creative evolution (trans: Mitchell A). Macmillan, London

Bergson H (1914) The problem of personality, first lecture. In: Bergson at the University of Edinburgh 100 years ago. https://www.blogs.hss.ed.ac.uk/crag/2014/12/18/bergson-at-the-university-of-edinburgh-100-years-ago/

Bergson H (1932) Les deux sources de la morale et de la religion. Félix Alcan, Paris. In: Bergson H (1935) The two sources of moralinty and religion (trans: Audra RA, Brereton C). Macmillan, London

Bistis M (1996) Managing Bergson's crowd: professionalism and the 'mondain' at the Collège de France. Hist Reflect 22:389–406

Canales J (2005) Einstein, Bergson, and the experiment that failed: intellectual cooperation at the League of Nations. Mod Lang Notes 120(5):1168–1191

Davis NZ (1988) 'Any resemblance to persons living or dead': film and the challenge of authenticity. Hist J Film Radio Telev 8(3):269–283

Deleuze G (1983) L'image-mouvement, In: Deleuze G (1986) Cinema I: The movement-image (trans: Tomlinson H, Habberjam B). Athlone, London

Deleuze G (1985) L'image-temps, In: DeleuzeG (1989) Cinema II: The time-image (trans: Tomlinson H, Galeta R). University Minnesota Press, Minneapolis

Doherty TP (1999) Pre-code Hollywood: sex, immorality, and insurrection in American cinema, 1930–1934. Columbia University Press, New York

Dorr RLC (1917) Inside the Russian revolution. Macmillan, New York

Durozoi G (2002) History of the surrealist movement (trans: Anderson A). University of Chicago Press, Chicago

European Union (2000) Charter of fundamental rights of the European Union, 2000/C 364/01

Foucault M (1976) Two lectures. In Foucault M (1980) Power/knowledge: selected interviews and other writings, 1972–1977 (ed Gordon C, trans: Gordon C et al). Harvester, London, pp 78–108

Fougerol H (1913) La figure humaine et le droit (The human face and the law)

France (1978) Loi n° 78–17 du 6 Janvier 1978 relative à l'informatique, aux fichiers et aux libertés. Journal officiel du 7 janvier 1978 et rectificatif au J.O. du 25 janvier 1978

---

[86] Eg *Case C-18/18 Eva Glawischnig-Piesczek v Facebook Ireland Limited*, CJEU (Third Chamber), 3 October 2019.

[87] Eg *Von Hannover v Germany* (Third Division) [2004] EMLR 379; (2005) 40 EHRR 1 (ECtHR third Div); *Von Hannover v Germany (No 2)* (2012) 55 EHRR 15 (ECtHR Grand Chamber).

Georges-Michel M (1914) Henri Bergson nous parle du cinéma (Henri Bergson talks to us about cinema). Le J

Gilman SL (1988) Klabund (4 November 1890–14 August 1928). In: German Fiction Writers, 1885–1913 (ed Hardin JN) vol. 66. Dictionary of literary biography, pp 251–257

Herring E (2019, May 6) Henri Bergson, celebrity (ed Warburton N). Aeon. https://aeon.co/essays/henri-bergson-the-philosopher-damned-for-his-female-fans

Hobsbawm E (1994) The age of extremes: the short twentieth century, 1914–1991. Michael Joseph, London

Illustrated London News (1911, June 3) Philosophy as fashionable as the wedding: the Parisiennes' whim. Illustrated London News, Summer Leaves (Supplement), p 849

James W (1878) Remarks on Spencer's definition of mind as correspondence. J Specul Philos 12(1):1–18

Kahn EL (1984) The neglected majority: 'les camoufleurs', art history, and World War I. University Press of America, Lanham

Klabund (Alfred Henschke) (1929) Rasputin. Phaidon, Wein

Kolb S (2019) There is no progress: change is all we know Nordic. J Aesthet 57–58:87–1085

Lake J (2016) The face that launched a thousand lawsuits: the American women who forged a right to privacy. Yale University Press, New Haven

Lang W, Davenport D (1925, November 16) The Red Kimona (writ Adela Rogers St. Johns, intro Davenport D/Mrs. Wallace Reid)

Lefebvre A (2018) Human rights and the care of the self. Duke University Press, Durham

Llewellyn K (1936) On warranty of quality, and society. Colum L Rev 36(5):699–744

Mare A (1916) Carnet 5, Camp des Oyes

Marinetti FT (1909, February 10) Manifesto del futurismo (The founding and manifesto of futurism). Le Figaro

McGrath L (2013) Bergson comes to America. J Hist Ideas 74(4):599–620

Metzinger J (1911, August 16) 'Cubisme' et Tradition. Paris-Journal

Mill JS (1859) On liberty. In Mill JS (1962) John Stuart Mill: Utilitarianism, on liberty, essay on Bentham, together with selected writings of Jeremy Bentham and John Austin (ed and intro Warnock M). Collins, London, pp 126–250

Mitchell P (2015) A history of tort law 1900–1950. Cambridge University Press, Cambridge

Morsink J (2021) Article by article: the Universal Declaration of Human Rights for a new generation. University of Pennsylvania Press, Philadelphia

Nelson G, Wright H (1945) Tomorrow's house: a complete guide for the home-builder. Simon and Schuster, New York

New York Times (1926, December 13), Pictures cut up by artist, restored and sold; puzzled French painter sues to regain them, p 4

Pruitt LR (2004) Her own good name: two centuries of talk about chastity. Md L Rev 63(3):401–539

Regulation (EU) 2016/679 of the European Parliament and of the Council of 27 April 2016 on the protection of natural persons with regard to the processing and on the free movement of such data, and repealing Directive 95/46/EC (GDPR)

Syed SG (2016) The right to destroy under droit d'auteur: a theoretical moral right or a tool of art speech? Chi-Kent J Intell Prop 15(2):504–537

The Times (1911, October 21) Professor Bergson on the soul. The Times, p 4

The Times (1934a, February 28) High Court of Justice, p 4

The Times (1934b, March 1) High Court of Justice, p 4

The Times (1934c, March 6) High Court of Justice, p 5

United Nations General Assembly (1948, December 10) Universal Declaration of Human Rights. Res 217 A(III)

Wagner WJ (1970) The right to one's own likeness in French Law. Ind L J 46(1):1–36

Warren SD, Brandeis LD (1890) The right to privacy. Harv L Rev 4(5):193–220

Yusupov F (1927), Rasputin: his malignant influence and his assassination (trans: Rayner O). Jonathan Cape, London

# Chapter 5
# Reappraisal

**Abstract** This chapter reflects back on the ways of ideas about human rights to privacy and contiguous rights over data and memory in modern times. It suggests that, if human rights are necessary mechanisms to keep humans within society, then we need to pay attention to common human understandings of privacy and contiguous rights, learning from the subjugated knowledges of the past. The illuminations offered in this book's investigations are still quite vague. Yet they anticipate in surprising ways 'new' ways of thinking around privacy and contiguous rights in more recent times.

**Keywords** Privacy · Identity · Rights · Modern · Universal declaration

As I note in this book, one of the many tragic losses that occurred with the first and second world law along with their attendant diseases was the intellectual loss associated with the death or marginalisation of some of the most interesting and creative thinkers of modern times. In practical terms, the impact was inevitable when it came to drafting of the Universal Declaration in 1948 as a modern human rights instrument looking to the reassert 'the dignity and worth of the human person' and create the foundations for a better life.[1] No doubt the compressed time frame for agreeing the terms of the Declaration made deeper consensus even for those at the table more difficult, even apart from the problem of locating and understanding ideas of others that were either long forgotten or never really known outside a small community of devotees. But in a post-war United Nations bent on fashioning a human rights declaration that would 'reaffirm[] their faith in fundamental human rights',[2] we might have expected to have seen some greater appreciation of Hannah Arendt's fleeting sense of privacy in transient refugee communities as about friendship, sympathy and love, Franz Kafka's reflections on the mechanistically bureaucratic ways of the modern metropolis, and Henri Bergson's ideas of the possibility of creative

---

[1] Universal Declaration (1948), Preamble, fifth recital.

[2] Ibid.

M. Richardson, *The Right to Privacy 1914–1948*, SpringerBriefs in Law,
https://doi.org/10.1007/978-981-99-4498-9_5

evolution resisting cinematic mechanism along with the mechanism of other modern communications technologies and practices – just to give some examples.

While I was writing these final words, I was watching Charlie Chaplin's brilliant 1936 film *Modern Times*,[3] and reading his biography where he mentions meeting a young journalist on the New York *World* and hearing his harrowing story of the Detroit car industry 'luring healthy young men off the farms who, after four or five years at the belt system, became nervous wrecks'.[4] Others have pointed to his meeting with Mahatma Gandhi where they talked about Gandhi's abhorrence of machines as another inspiration.[5] It is a film that bears some marked resemblances to Kafka's early tragicomedy *America*, where the young Karl Rossmann is 'packed off' by his parents to America and becomes employed for a time as a liftboy in hotel Occidental, working long hours under the autocratic rein of the Head Waiter and sleeping in a dormitory with other lift-boys.[6] Both of these stories offer intriguing perspectives on the position of marginalised and excluded individuals in the face of what Georg Simmel called 'the external culture and technique of [modern] life'.[7] But they are also replete with novel and interesting ideas about how to maintain a sense of human identity in the face of its relentless mechanism – in the case of Chaplin's 'factory worker'/'Little Tramp', for instance, by having a nervous breakdown, falling in love, breaking the law, and escaping to the open road with his 'gamin' ally (Paulette Goddard). And in the case of Kafka's lift-boy Karl by joining a motley group of travelling players and moving west, outside the boundaries of civilised society.

If, as Arendt argues, modern human rights are necessary mechanisms to keep marginalised humans within society,[8] then we need to pay attention to their understandings of these rights, learning from what Michel Foucault might call their 'subjugated knowledges'[9] – for instance, the deficiencies of the modern factory system including its surveillance technologies and repetitive mechanised exploitation of workers that Chaplin's worker struggled under and escaped in *Modern Times*, the unfairness and oppressiveness of the modern capitalist bureaucratic system that Kafka's lift-boy struggled under and escaped in *Amerika*. Likewise, we need to pay attention to those who tell their stories, who may be or become marginalised in turn – as with Arendt the Jewish refugee, Kafka the little-known German-Jewish writer, Bergson the out-of-fashion French-Jewish philosopher, and Chaplin the English-born street performer turned Hollywood star who was excluded from the US after the second world war because of his supposed communist sympathies on display in films like *Modern Times*.[10] The illuminations they offer are still quite

[3] Chaplin (1936).

[4] Chaplin (1936) p. 383.

[5] Desai (2019).

[6] Kafka (1914).

[7] Simmel (1903).

[8] Arendt (1949) p. 34.

[9] Foucault (1976).

[10] Sbardellati and Shaw (2003) quoting from FBI memo no 100–127090-186.

vague. Yet they anticipated in surprising ways 'new' ways of thinking around privacy and contiguous rights such as the right to data protection, to rectification and erasure in more recent times. And, if they go some way in guiding us on how to do rights better in the present and future (as well as giving insight into the past), all the better.

# References

Arendt H (1949) 'The rights of man': what are they? Modern Rev 3(1):24–36

Chaplin C (1936) Modern times. United Artists, Hollywood

Desai N (2019, October 10) Gandhiji inspired Charlie Chaplin to make his classic movie 'Modern Times'. The Leaflet, https://theleaflet.in/gandhiji-inspired-charlie-chaplin-to-make-his-classic-movie-modern-times/

Foucault M (1976) Two lectures. In Foucault M (1980), Power/knowledge: selected interviews and other writings, 1972–1977 (ed Gordon C, trans: Gordon C et al). Harvester, London, pp 78–108

Kafka F (1914) Amerika. In: Kafka F (1996) Amerika: the man who disappeared: the new translation (trans: Hofmann M). Penguin, London

Sbardellati J, Shaw T (2003) Booting a tramp: Charlie Chaplin, the FBI, and the construction of the subversive image in Red Scare America. Pac Hist Rev 72(4):495–530

Simmel G (1903) The metropolis and mental life (Die großstädte und das geistesleben). In: Simmel G (1991) On individuality and social forms (ed Levine DN). University of Chicago Press, Chicago, pp 324–339

United Nations General Assembly (1948, December 10) Universal Declaration of Human Rights. Res 217 A(III)

Printed in the United States
by Baker & Taylor Publisher Services